Fatal Fortune

Fatal Fortune

The Death of Chicago's Millionaire Orphan

Virginia A. McConnell

PRAEGER

Westport, Connecticut
London

Library of Congress Cataloging-in-Publication Data

McConnell, Virginia A., 1942–
    Fatal fortune : the death of Chicago's millionaire orphan / Virginia A.
  McConnell.
        p. cm.
    Includes bibliographical references and index.
    ISBN 0–275–98473–7 (alk. paper)
    1. McClintock, William, d. 1924. 2. Shepherd, William
Darling. 3. Homicide—Illinois—Chicago—Case studies. 4. Millionaires—
Crimes against—Illinois—Chicago—Case studies. 5. Trials (Murder)—
Illinois—Chicago. I. Title.
HV6534.C4M33   2005
364.152′3′0977311—dc22   2005018654

British Library Cataloguing in Publication Data is available.

Library of Congress Catalog Card Number: 2005018654
ISBN: 0–275–98473–7

First published in 2005

Praeger Publishers, 88 Post Road West, Westport, CT 06881
An imprint of Greenwood Publishing Group, Inc.
www.praeger.com

Printed in the United States of America

∞™

The paper used in this book complies with the
Permanent Paper Standard issued by the National
Information Standards Organization (Z39.48–1984).

10 9 8 7 6 5 4 3 2 1

Everyone should have at least one brother. Older or younger, they can always be counted on for assistance, advice, reality checks, and good-natured teasing. I am lucky in that I have three: Mike McConnell, Matt McConnell, and my brother-in-law Bill Greer.

Contents

Photo-essay follows page 90.

Acknowledgments

A project like this can never be accomplished without help from a lot of people. In no particular order, I'd like to thank:

Lori Loseth for letting me pick her brain about bacterial DNA.

Charity Goodell for risking the wrath of the Homeland Security police by researching typhoid as a biological weapon.

Samantha McCluskey for her terrific research on Dorothy Ellingson.

Sergeant Joshua Macey, USMC, for his research on mercury.

The family of Isabelle Pope for sharing the pictures, effects, and memories of their mother.

The very helpful folks at the Ouray County Historical Society: Ginny Harrington, Glenda Moore, and Ann Hoffman.

Shirley Noland at the University of Michigan Law School Registrar's Office for digging until she found Carl Sigfrid Peterson's record.

Julie Hansen at William Penn University in Oskaloosa, Iowa, for the information on the Oskaloosa College scandal.

Karen Klinkenberg at the University of Minnesota Archives for information on Charles Faiman's one semester there.

Sarah Hartwell at the Dartmouth College Library Archives for the transcript and information about Billy McClintock.

Anne Malley at New Trier Township High School for the graduation material on Billy and Isabelle.

Piriya Metcalfe at the Chicago Historical Society for her generosity and incredible service.

Sharon Bruce at Bethany College for information on the Grafs and Emma Nelson.

As always, our wonderful college librarian, Jackson Vance Matthews, for her aid and support.

And my editor, Heather Staines, who steers me in the right direction when I get off course and nurtures me with positive comments.

Introduction

In the twenty years I have been familiar with this case, the biggest mystery to me is why nobody has ever written about it. The McClintock-Shepherd saga could not have been performed against a more colorful background or with a more colorful cast of characters.

Jazz Age Chicago teemed with personality. It also teemed with quite a bit of violence, and the possible typhoid poisoning of a young millionaire must have seemed pretty tame in comparison. Prohibition was in effect, and as a result, organized crime was having a field day. Nearly every newspaper edition carried some account of a gangland attack as the various mob families vied for power in Chicago. Johnny Torrio, Bugs Moran, Al Capone, Dion O'Banion, the Genna brothers—they're all here, sharing space with the investigation into the suspicious death of Billy McClintock.

Nathan Leopold and Richard Loeb are here, too, having just gone through their sentencing hearing in the summer of 1924. They pop up on occasion in reports from Joliet Prison, where they were working on sentences of life plus ninety-nine years. The same prosecutorial crew took on the Shepherd case, and in the same courtroom.

It was a time of union start-ups, and the violence that attended those birth pangs overflows into our story in the persons of witness Patrick McMahon and the jury briber James Callan. It was an era when people actually called each other "dirty rat"—and meant it!—and didn't hesitate to knock the other fellow down when they felt insulted.

This is a story of young love tragically thwarted, with the image of a desperate fiancee going by herself to get a marriage license, only to be turned away by the greedy guardians who wanted to prevent a deathbed wedding. It's a story of con artists—not only the one who ran a diploma mill but the guardians themselves, who lived by sponging off others. It is a story of an "avenging fury," a judge who fought against all odds to get justice for Billy and his mother; and it is a story of a cursed inheritance, a Fatal Fortune that killed everyone who got it.

People in the 1920s had trouble seeing how anyone could infect another with germs. We who live in the post-9/11 world, however, have no difficulty grasping that possibility. Bioterrorism was not even a remote consideration in the America of the Jazz Age.

In 1925, people were reading Fitzgerald, Hemingway, dos Passos, Cather, Dreiser, Woolf, Eliot, Pound, Glasgow—it was the golden age of American literature. They danced to the music of Louis Armstrong, Duke Ellington, and Bix Beiderbecke. They thrilled to movies starring Fatty Arbuckle, Ronald Colman, Vilma Banky, Charlie Chaplin, Rudolph Valentino, and Norma Talmadge. They agonized over the eighteen-day plight of Floyd Collins, trapped in a Kentucky cave, and followed the Scopes "Monkey" Trial. They cheered for Red Grange and Jim Thorpe in football, Bill Tilden and Helen Wills in tennis, Babe Ruth and Lou Gehrig in baseball, and Bobby Jones in golf. What a year!

Naturally, in any murder trial, there will be testimony at variance with other testimony as people put their own spins on events, place themselves in the spotlight or in the shadows, tell deliberate lies, or genuinely misremember what really happened. I have chosen to present as true the testimony of Charles Faiman, the primary witness against William Shepherd, because I believe that, at least in its major aspects, it *is* true. Faiman, who seems to have lived his entire life pulling some scam or other, had absolutely nothing to gain and everything to lose—including his freedom and possibly his life—by telling this story. After all, if the jury believed him, he, too, would be found guilty of the murder of Billy McClintock as an accomplice. Other witnesses, some of whom he did not know, also corroborated him.

In many ways, this case was frustrating because of a lack of follow-up, or follow-up that was not reported. When someone related a version of a statement or event, there was no apparent questioning of others who were there as to whether it came down that way or not. At the trial, for example, there was an issue as to what Faiman said he gave Shepherd in those vials—yet Faiman himself wasn't asked to clarify. Servants in the McClintock-Shepherd household said that, on a specific day during Billy's illness, Mrs. Shepherd told them not to let Isabelle Pope into the house. Yet Isabelle testified that she *was* there on that day. So, were the servants mistaken about the day, or was Isabelle? Or did Mrs. Shepherd just change her mind? Such discrepancies were never resolved.

There were several different reports of the actual worth of the "million-dollar estate," some putting it as high as $7 million. Although many articles had it at $2 million or $3 million, it seems to have been about half that (depending on the real estate valuation, which might have made it closer to seven figures) at the time of Billy's death. But that was close enough for the newspapers to use the romantic reference of "Millionaire Orphan." The Fatal Fortune itself was probably never as high as a million until Billy's father increased it with his real estate investments in the early years of the twentieth century.

William Nelson McClintock, his fiancee Isabelle Pope, and the Shepherds all spelled his nickname as "Billie." In the newspapers, however, it was uniformly rendered as "Billy." Because of our contemporary association of "Billie" with the female name, I have chosen the more masculine version used by the newspapers.

I eliminated repetitious, nonprobative, or merely cumulative testimony. If a witness also appeared at the inquest, I give only a brief mention or summary during the trial section. Wherever there is quoted dialogue, it represents either the speaker's exact words or a close approximation.

All modern equivalents of money figures come from Economic History Services' database at http://eh.net/hmit/ppowerusd, titled "How Much Is That Worth Today?" This database converts figures from the past into 2003 values and can also compare the values of two past years. It is a wonderful tool that puts things into perspective for today's reader. For example, when we learn that the defendant paid a witness $50 for information, it doesn't sound like much—just a little weekend spending money. But when we realize that it would equal today's figure of $550, we see how incriminating this payment was. He must have wanted this information very badly indeed; and, since money is at the very root of this case, as it so often is with crime, I felt it was important to show readers these equivalent values throughout the book.

In presenting the story of the death of Billy McClintock, I wanted to bring this raucous, vibrant era to life, as well as the people involved in the case itself. Even if there were no murder, the characters alone would be worth the excursion. I hope you agree.

Chapter 1

The Fatal Fortune

Do you realize, darling boy, that in loving you more than all else in this world, it would kill me if anything happened to you?
—Isabelle Pope

"Billy, honey, you're burning up!" Isabelle Pope had just taken her fiance's temperature and watched it climb to 102.5 degrees. "Let me drive you home." It was the Sunday before Thanksgiving, November 23, 1924.[1]

But Billy McClintock did not want to go home. He wanted to stay in Wilmette with Isabelle and her family, where he had come to visit after dinner that day so the two young people could plan their February wedding. Although he lived in nearby Kenilworth, a wealthy suburb of Chicago, he frequently stayed for several days with the Popes so that he and Isabelle could work out the logistics of what promised to be a big society affair.

William Nelson McClintock and Isabelle Pope, both twenty-one, belonged to well-to-do families, with Billy being an actual millionaire as the result of an inheritance from his deceased parents. Although he lived in a large, magnificent house with many servants, Billy was unspoiled by it all. He was popular and fun to be with, and he retained a kind of simplicity that was unusual in one who had been wealthy his whole life. Isabelle's father, Henry A. Pope, had made his money in sales and invested it wisely: the Pope family lived in an impressive home in tony Wilmette, and their four children all went to college.

Billy spent a lot of time with his friends, who enjoyed dinners, dancing, card games, and billiards. It was the Roaring Twenties, after all, and these children of privilege took every advantage of an era that emphasized good times. At his home in Kenilworth, Billy switched his large bedroom with his small den, preferring to have room for a pool table for his friends to enjoy.[2] He had his own automobile and was generous about driving people around, although he tended to exceed the speed limit (he once knocked a young piano tuner off his bicycle at an intersection).[3] This behavior was quite a change for the little boy who had been subject to what were termed "nervous attacks" and whose frequent illnesses as a child were attributed to this condition.[4]

Isabelle and Billy both attended New Trier Township High School in Winnetka. New Trier, which opened in 1901, has always had a reputation as one of the top high schools in the United States. Its students, numbering 3,800 in 2003, come from the surrounding wealthy North Shore communities, and over 90 percent of them matriculate at four-year colleges after graduation.[5]

Billy and Isabelle began dating in the spring of 1920, at the end of their junior year. He was attracted to her classic good looks—deep blue eyes and blonde hair—and her effervescent personality. From that time on, they saw each other at least once a day, and more often two or three times. In the newspaper issue for the Class of 1921, Billy was described as "a true disciple of the Pope," an in-joke for all who knew them. Isabelle was voted "Most Graceful Girl," and the list of her activities shows that she had enough energy for all of them: the Elizabethan Society, Glee Club, Dramatic Club, captain of the basketball team, Music Club, French Club, Social Committee, and Girls' Club. Billy's list was impressive but more subdued: House of Representatives, Chemistry Club, Student Council, and captain of the Cadet Corps (a sort of Junior ROTC).[6]

In an era when most high school graduates did not go on to college, the New Trier Class of 1921's plans reflect the upper-class status of its members: Harvard, Yale, Stanford, University of Illinois, Mount Holyoke, Michigan, Beloit, Dartmouth (Billy), Northwestern (Isabelle).[7] One of their classmates at New Trier was the actor Ralph Bellamy. He thought Isabelle was so good at dancing that she should study it at Northwestern, but she had always wanted to be a teacher. To her, dancing was for fun, not for a career.[8]

At Northwestern, Isabelle joined the Alpha Phi sorority, whose notable members include Lady Bird Johnson's press secretary, Liz Carpenter, and actress Jeri Ryan. At Dartmouth, Billy pledged at the Phi Delta Theta fraternity, whose alumni include Neil Armstrong, Roger Ebert, Burt Reynolds, and Frank Lloyd Wright.[9] The two young people corresponded almost daily, and Billy frequently called Isabelle from Dartmouth. During vacations, they were inseparable. They bought records together and listened to them over and over.[10] (Some popular songs from 1924 are familiar to twenty-first-century listeners: "Somebody Loves Me"; "Indian Love Call"; "Rose Marie"; "I'll See You in My Dreams"; "Deep in My Heart, Dear"; "I Want to Be Happy"; and "California, Here I Come.") They went to movies starring Douglas Fairbanks, Rudolph Valentino, Adolph Menjou, and Mary Astor. They danced the Charleston, the Shimmy, and the Black Bottom.[11] They went to baseball games at Cubs Park (to be rechristened Wrigley Field a few years later) to see Isabelle's favorite team.[12]

But Billy did not fare well at Dartmouth. He was doing too much partying and not enough classwork and was placed on academic probation all three years of his matriculation there. When he reached the end of his junior year, he did not have enough credits to graduate with his class (1925). His transcript shows grades of C, D, and E (the equivalent of F), with one lone course (History I during his freshman year) earning a B. He failed English II, took it again, and received only a D. He failed Zoology I and got a C the second time. Billy did not have a single A grade in his six semesters of attendance.[13]

Billy dropped out of Dartmouth after his junior year in June 1924 (he had promised Isabelle he would go back to college "unless there is no chance for a degree, which would then make such a thing foolish,"[14] but he must have known even as he told her this that he could not possibly graduate on time) and returned to Kenilworth to attend business school in Chicago. He wanted to be closer to Isabelle, and he fully intended to take over his estate, which he had inherited that April when he turned twenty-one. He was hoping that Isabelle would consent to an earlier wedding than the projected date of June 1925, but she had just landed her first contract, as kindergarten teacher at the Hawthorne School in Glencoe, and wanted to complete the semester there.

Billy and Isabelle were constantly together during this time. Every morning he drove to her home so she could take him to the commuter train for his business classes in downtown Chicago. Then she drove his car to her teaching job in Glencoe, picked him up at the train station at one o'clock, and had lunch with him. More often than not they would spend the rest of the afternoon together and part of the evening as well.

Although Isabelle had begun her education at Northwestern in 1921, she decided after her freshman year to enroll instead in the Pestalozzi-Froebel Teachers College in Chicago because she wanted to get her teaching certificate sooner rather than later. Pestalozzi-Froebel opened in 1896 (Froebel was the educator who had coined the term "kindergarten") and would eventually close its doors in 1971. Probably its most well-known instructor was the author Saul Bellow, who taught there from 1938–1942.[15]

Dedicated and ambitious, Isabelle also took summer courses at Columbia University while she was at Pestalozzi-Froebel.[16] It had long been the practice (oftentimes written into a teacher's contract) that marriage meant the loss of a teaching position, and Isabelle had worked hard to get where she was. She wasn't ready to give it up before she even got a chance to try it out. So she and Billy compromised on February 22, 1925, as their wedding date.

A look at some of the many letters written back and forth between Billy and Isabelle while he was at Dartmouth reveals a young couple very much in love and extremely committed to spending the rest of their lives together.[17] In April 1924, after he got back to college from his spring break, Billy wrote:

> Darling girl, I am just nearly all in. This leaving you this time has taken all the nerve I have.
>
> Sweetheart, it will be so very wonderful to have you wearing my ring and every one with full knowledge of the fact of our love and intention to marry as soon as we can.
>
> Precious, there is no news, so you will have to listen to me rave a bit, for my heart and all of me is just overflowing for the love of you.
>
> O, darling, don't for one moment ever think I don't realize how lucky I am to have you for my bride.

And from Isabelle:

> Three—one, two, three letters from you today. Oh, how happy I am to have such a wonderful, faithful boy in love with me. Whatever have I done to deserve you?

Liz [Isabelle's sister] is downstairs playing the [V]ictrola. She's playing all the records we bought together and that we played together so many times. You are so closely linked in my mind with those records that when I hear them I feel all choked up in my throat. O, sweetheart, I want you and need you so. I can hardly stand this being apart. I can't write more. I love you and am all your own.

What a wonderful letter from you today. I have been just bubbling over with happiness all day just because of it. O, how I love you! If you were here this minute I'd give you such a big hug you'd cry for mercy.

My own darling boy, Excuse that overflow of emotion, darling, but that's just the way I feel tonight—just overflowing with love of you.... My heart is sick with longing for you.

When Isabelle went to Dartmouth for Billy's Winter Carnival weekend during his freshman year, she made a big hit with his friends, and this impressed Billy. He wrote to Mr. and Mrs. Pope, unable to conceal his growing devotion: "I am adoring her more every minute. Excuse me if I wax emotional, but it is hard to repress my feelings." For her part, Isabelle noticed that Billy was getting a big thumbs-up from her own friends and relatives: "Everyone has fallen for him," she wrote her parents that same weekend, "and Eleanor and Cookie are crazy about him." She thought Billy comported himself as a complete gentleman: "I never realized before how very proper and conventional he is."[18]

Even though he had dropped out of Dartmouth, Billy still considered himself connected to his former school. He followed the football team's magical 1924 season, where they went undefeated, with only one tie to mar their record, and were ranked tenth in the nation.[19] On October 18, he went to New Haven for the Dartmouth-Yale game, the one that resulted in the tie.

Billy had been feeling ill throughout November, although that didn't stop him much from his usual round of activities—except for his classes at the business college. Never much of a student, Billy skipped the classes during his illness, but not the card parties or going out with Isabelle. He rarely returned before three o'clock in the morning, and when he was attending classes he was out again by eight. It was probably not the best lifestyle for a young man who had been sickly in his childhood.[20]

That Sunday, November 23, Isabelle convinced her fiance that, with such a high fever, he belonged home and in bed. She drove

Billy's car to the house on Melrose Avenue that he shared with his guardians, William Darling ("Darl") Shepherd and his wife Julie, and saw to it that he went up to his room. Isabelle stayed downstairs to talk with the Shepherds, who were entertaining guests from Albuquerque in what they called their "radio room": Mrs. Mildred Davidson, newly widowed; and Mrs. Davidson's unmarried sister, Ruby Peel.

In the evening Darl Shepherd drove Isabelle back to her home at 910 Lake Avenue in Wilmette. On the way, he spoke to her of an oddly intimate subject: Billy's bowels! Billy was careless in this matter, he said, because he was frequently busy doing something (and presumably didn't stop to relieve himself when he should) and didn't always eat the right things. He had a tendency to get constipated, so Shepherd regularly gave him a laxative. In fact, he had given him one that very night. Shepherd seemed to be instructing Isabelle to continue this practice after their marriage: "We who love him must take care of him in this way." Isabelle thought it a strange and embarrassing conversation.

The next day, Monday, Isabelle hurried over to the Kenilworth house after teaching in Glencoe. Billy was no better—actually, he was worse—and he talked to her about getting married right then. The Shepherds had gotten married when Darl was on his supposed deathbed, and Darl always claimed this was what cured him. Billy thought it might work for him as well, and Isabelle wanted to have the legal right to take him to the South for a cure.

By Tuesday, November 25, Billy's flu-like symptoms had not abated. Concerned, attending physician Dr. Rufus Stolp called in a private nurse, who arrived the next day. Isabelle visited both days, but Billy was experiencing some delirium at this point. On Thursday, Thanksgiving Day, she was allowed in the room in the morning, but Julie Shepherd forbade her to go into Billy's room in the afternoon. Isabelle stood out in the hallway with the flowers she had brought to cheer up her fiance. On Friday, she was allowed to stay in Billy's room for half an hour, but had to stay six feet away from the bed.

Julie was bossy in regulating who could see Billy and for how long, and Isabelle sometimes had the feeling she would be happier if she, Isabelle, stopped coming to visit. Julie bragged that Billy wouldn't take food from anyone but herself, but she was so omnipresent that once when Isabelle was in the sickroom, Billy harshly told Julie to leave them alone.

When Billy was well, he had to share his room with his step-father, William Shepherd. It was an odd arrangement, as Julie had a very large bedroom and Billy's was very small. This was his own choice, of course, because he wanted a big den/game room, but it would seem that in that large house there could have been an alternative arrangement for Shepherd, who claimed his wife had kicked him out of the bedroom because he snored. But wouldn't his snoring keep Billy awake as well? Shepherd took the single bed closest to the door, so he always knew when Billy came in at night. Isabelle got the feeling that the older couple had set this up to spy on their ward.[21]

As time went on, Dr. Stolp began to suspect that his patient might have typhoid fever: every day he grew worse, with a higher temperature, delirium, and high pulse and respiration. On Saturday, November 29, Stolp consulted with a typhoid special-ist, Dr. James B. Herrick, who performed a Widal test on Billy's blood. The results would be confirmed on Monday, December 1: Billy had typhoid fever.

Today, typhoid fever is rare except in developing countries. The few hundred cases that occur in the United States each year occur mostly in those who have been traveling in areas where typhoid is still a serious threat. With modern antibiotics, patients usually recover in a few weeks. The symptoms of typhoid fever remain the same as in Billy McClintock's day: high fever (often as high as 103 degrees, which is what Billy's was), headache, stomach pains, and either constipation (mostly in adults) or diar-rhea (mostly in children). In more serious cases, like Billy's, the patient will experience delirium and intestinal hemorrhaging.[22]

When Dr. Stolp first thought of typhoid (the wonder is that it took him so long, as there was something of an outbreak on the North Shore), he asked Billy if he had eaten any shellfish recently. Billy told him he had last eaten raw oysters, a par-ticular favorite of his, on November 3 at the newly constructed Windermere House in Chicago.

The original Windermere Hotel had been built a few years before the Columbian Exposition of 1892, held in Chicago. The Windermere House, where Billy ate in November, had just been completed in 1923, and that was why the young people wanted to eat there. The new building, sometimes mistakenly referred to as the Windermere Hotel, had two restaurants: the Anchorage and the Classic Room. The old Windermere Hotel was torn down in the 1950s, but the Windermere House still stands. It is now an apartment complex, with a one-bedroom, one-bathroom studio going for $1,100 a month—equivalent to a healthy mortgage payment.[23]

Of the foursome who dined at the Windermere House on November 3, 1924—Billy, Isabelle, Isabelle's cousin Dudley "Dud" Pope, and his fiancee Virginia "Jimmie" Buell—all had eaten oysters except Isabelle, but only Billy got typhoid.

When Isabelle visited Billy that Saturday, the day Dr. Herrick was called in, he was very sick and very uncomfortable. She was allowed in the sickroom for only three minutes, but she stayed at the Kenilworth home all day. At that time she talked to Darl Shepherd about getting a marriage license so she could afterward take Billy to the South to convalesce. Their original honeymoon was supposed to be in Europe, but Isabelle didn't care about that. She just wanted Billy to get better.

But Shepherd was not encouraging. He admitted that Billy had asked him about getting a marriage license, but he told his ward, and now told Isabelle, that the law required both parties to be present when applying for it. Isabelle might have accepted that, but she remembered that her brother-in-law had gotten a license without her sister. "Well, it's a new law in this state," Shepherd told her. "Besides, as I told Billy, it wouldn't be fair to you to do it this way. You want a nice wedding, not a hurried-up death-bed one."

Isabelle told Shepherd she didn't need a big wedding, and reminded him of the oft-told story of his own deathbed wedding and subsequent cure. "I think Mrs. Shepherd regrets not having had a big wedding," he said. "When people have a big wedding, everyone remembers their anniversary with flowers and congratulations, but when you are married this way, no one ever knows. You always have to remind people that it is your anniversary."

On Sunday, Isabelle came back to the McClintock-Shepherd home, but was not allowed to see Billy, who at this point was in and out of delirium. Once again, she spent the day there, talking with the Shepherds and hoping Billy would show signs of getting better. A second nurse had been called in, and the two were caring for him around the clock.

Darl Shepherd seemed particularly animated that day. He entertained them with stories and jokes; told them he had gotten London on the radio; talked of scientific advances; and related what a vaudeville fortune-teller had once predicted for Julie's cousin Carl Sigfrid, a Colorado lawyer: that he was in love with someone he had known long ago, but would never marry her. This was supposedly Billy's mother, Emma McClintock, who had once dated Sigfrid before her marriage to William McClintock Sr.

At one point on that Sunday, after typhoid was suspected, Isabelle and Darl Shepherd sat together on the front porch. He related how Billy had come to him for some pills about a week before he got sick (Shepherd seems to have been a dispensing druggist for all his friends and relatives). "Boy, are you sick?" Shepherd had asked him, and Billy replied, "I am coming down with typhoid." Shepherd thought this meant Billy knew where he had gotten it, and suspected it might have been when he went to New Haven for the Dartmouth-Yale game. He had eaten oysters at a restaurant in New York City, and there was an epidemic there at the time. (Shepherd said the Dartmouth-Yale game had been played on November 15, but in fact it was on October 18, too far away from the sixteen-to-eighteen-day incubation period.)

Shepherd went on to tell Isabelle that he had made quite a study of typhoid and of germs in general. What he did not explain, however, was why—if he and Billy had had a conversation about typhoid a full week before Billy became ill, and if he had made such a study of the disease as he claimed—he did not tell Dr. Stolp about this. If the Widal test had been performed early on, perhaps the antidote would have been effective. If Shepherd thought Billy might have had typhoid, why did he give him a laxative, when that was the worst thing a typhoid patient could have? Since constipation is one of the telltale symptoms of typhoid fever, and since Billy supposedly confided in his guardian that he suspected he had that disease, why would Shepherd thoughtlessly give him a cathartic? The answer, of course, is that Billy most likely did *not* know that he had typhoid and never made any such statement. But Darl Shepherd knew it.

Dr. Stolp, who attended Billy every day from the onset of his illness on Sunday, November 23, stated that Billy never said anything to him about having typhoid.[24] Isabelle, who had been with him several times a day throughout that whole period from the beginning of November, likewise never heard anything about typhoid from Billy. He had been feeling ill the night of the Windermere House dinner, yet went ahead and ordered oysters anyway—so he couldn't have thought he had contracted typhoid from the oysters he ate two weekends before at the Yale game or he would have avoided them.

An officer of the Northern Trust, Lewis McArthur, had the same experience. Darl Shepherd had gone there to tell them that Billy was too ill to sign checks and the household needed money. He told McArthur that Billy thought he had typhoid fever, and therefore he must know where he contracted it. Amelia Hall, Billy's first nurse, said the same thing, that Shepherd claimed Billy told him he had typhoid.[25] This was four or five days before typhoid was diagnosed and before Shepherd had said anything to Isabelle Pope about it. Nobody but Darl Shepherd ever claimed to have heard anything from Billy about his possibly having typhoid. And Darl Shepherd never passed this information along to Dr. Stolp.

Even if Billy *had* said this to Shepherd, what does it reveal about the latter's approach to his duties as caretaker of this young man? What parent, biological or adoptive, would fail to act on even a suspicion of such a serious illness? Shepherd's cavalier attitude toward Billy's alleged statement speaks volumes.

Isabelle took matters into her own hands, and on Monday afternoon she went down to City Hall and got a marriage license. As she suspected, Billy's presence was not required. Shepherd had lied to her, and probably to Billy as well. (He would later admit this, claiming that Billy really didn't want to get married on his deathbed and that he, Shepherd, made up the story so Billy could get out of it gracefully.)[26]

On Wednesday morning, when the notice appeared in the paper that Isabelle had applied for the marriage license, Darl Shepherd left his office early and hurried home. When Julie found out about the license, she was furious. She told a servant to lock the doors and not let Isabelle in, that she intended to have the young woman arrested for getting the license without Billy there. Then she called Isabelle's relatives and told them to keep her away from the Kenilworth home, as the doctor didn't want Billy disturbed—which was not true. (Afterward, the Shepherds would say that their cook was cranky and refused to fix extra meals, and that the nurses objected to Isabelle's reading of Billy's chart to him and getting him upset.)[27] But they must have relented, as Isabelle later said she was at the house that day.

Later that same day, Wednesday, December 3, Billy was unconscious and showing signs of intestinal hemorrhaging (bleeding through the nose, mouth, and gums). He had one of the most virulent forms of typhoid fever that Dr. Stolp had ever seen, and another physician would later comment that he had only seen one other case that severe.[28] Isabelle was not allowed in his room.

Despite the crisis in Billy's health, Darl Shepherd was expansive, upbeat, and joking as the Shepherds, Isabelle, Mrs. Pope, and the local pastor, Rev. Carl Naumann, gathered in Julie's bedroom. Darl told them about Typhoid Mary, who was a carrier of the disease, although not susceptible to it herself. He had followed this in the news, he said, because of a case he had. He recounted statistics regarding typhoid in the Spanish-American War and how those stats had improved by World War I because of antidotes. He seemed very knowledgeable about the disease and presented himself as something of an expert on it.

In the early hours of Thursday, December 4, Isabelle was informed that Billy was dying. She hurried over, at which time Dr. Stolp—who seemed to be waiting for her—did a final stethoscope examination and declared Billy dead at two thirty in the morning. The timing here indicates that possibly they already knew he was dead, and wanted Isabelle to be there so she could not later complain of being kept from his side. (One of the servants would later testify that Billy was already dead when Isabelle was summoned, although the death certificate gives 2:30 a.m. as the official time.)[29] She never got to use the marriage license.

The timing of Billy's death was unbelievably fortuitous for the Shepherds. Before Billy left Dartmouth, he had come home for a few days around his twenty-first birthday in April, and at that time executed a will drawn up for him by Darl Shepherd, who had an on-again, off-again law practice in downtown Chicago. It was to be an interim instrument, meant to protect his estate from the time he reached his majority until his marriage to Isabelle, and it named William Darling Shepherd as not only executor but sole beneficiary. The will provided for an annuity of $8,000 to Isabelle, but this was left entirely to the discretion of Shepherd. The reason for leaving Julie Shepherd out of the will? So she would be spared the burden of dealing with the estate.[30]

Was Shepherd aware that it is considered unethical for an attorney who is also a beneficiary to draw up a will? He claimed he was and that he informed Billy of this, but that Billy had insisted on Darl's representation of him.

Of course, once Billy and Isabelle married, this will would be null and void under Illinois law, superseded by the widow's rights in the event he did not make a new one. It was always Billy's intention, Shepherd claimed, to make this instrument a temporary one, a sort of bridge between turning twenty-one on

April 3 (and, of course, inheriting the estate) and getting married. But why not just leave the money directly to Isabelle in this will? Shepherd later said that Billy didn't want some other man spending his money if he should die before his marriage and Isabelle were to marry someone else.[31] But this sounds more like something Shepherd would come up with to convince Billy to make the "bridge" will and does not reflect the young man's personality at all. Billy would have wanted Isabelle to have his money regardless.

A servant in the Kenilworth home related that, on the day Billy died, Darl Shepherd was gloating about how they had fooled Isabelle and prevented her from marrying the young man.[32] Because if she had, the McClintock estate would have been hers, despite the will Billy had signed on his twenty-first birthday leaving everything to William Darling Shepherd. Under the terms of the trust set up by his mother, Billy had to be twenty-one in order to succeed to the estate. If the Shepherds were to inherit, then, Billy would have to die between April 3, 1924, and his wedding date, then set at February 22, 1925.

Billy's funeral on Saturday, December 6, 1924, was a sad affair. His pallbearers were the same young men who would have been groomsmen at his wedding: John Keith (his best man), Dudley Pope (Isabelle's cousin), Alfred McDougall, Howard Jones, James Snydacker, and Douglas Flood. Isabelle Pope, who was so distraught that she almost couldn't attend, fainted at the graveside.[33] Billy was buried next to his parents in Oak Woods Cemetery, one of Chicago's most historic burial grounds. (Those interred there include the former Mayor William Hale "Big Bill" Thompson, Olympic athlete Jesse Owens, physicist Enrico Fermi, baseball great Cap Anson, and crime boss "Big Jim" Colosimo.)[34]

Everyone agreed it was a tragedy, and many said it was a curse: so far, all the heirs of what was now being called the Fatal Fortune had come to an early end not long after inheriting it.[35]

An English nobleman had been the original inheritor of the estate. He died in about 1870 and left it to his widow, who then married a man named William Hickling. The nobleman's family ostracized the widow because Hickling was a commoner, so the Hicklings moved to America and settled in Ottawa, Illinois, not far from Chicago. Mrs. Hickling died only a few years after this, and the new heir William Hickling married Sarah Gensler, a woman almost thirty years his junior. Hickling died not long after they were married. There were hints and rumors that Sarah had hastened the passing of her husband with poison, but nothing came of it.

The story, a not very credible one, comes from a nurse in the Hickling home in the late 1870s, who claimed that when the seventy-five-year-old William Hickling was bedridden and ailing, his wife got him to make a will leaving everything to her. Shortly after he did so, she told him she knew someone who could cure him of his illness. A man purporting to be a doctor came to the house, gave Hickling some pills, and William died three days later. (This nurse also said that William McClintock was Mr. Hickling's private secretary, which was clearly untrue, as McClintock never met Sarah Hickling until she was already a widow.)

Now we come to the 1890s, when Sarah Gensler Hickling was a frail paralytic bound to a wheelchair. She went to Lemars, Iowa, to pay taxes on some property she held there, and met the county treasurer, William McClintock, a former schoolteacher. McClintock was a poor man but a popular and fun-loving one. He had recently broken his leg while ice-skating, and when Mrs. Hickling met him, he was in a cast and hobbling around on crutches.

It's difficult to see what might have attracted William McClintock to Mrs. Hickling, unless she was possessed of a sparkling personality. (A cynic, of course, would point out that, whatever her personality, she was certainly possessed of a lot of sparkling money.) She was about ten years his senior and bound to a wheelchair, whereas McClintock was very active and loved sports and dancing. Moreover, he was considered by the inhabitants of Lemars to be "a settled old bachelor." Nonetheless, in about 1895, McClintock married Mrs. Hickling and they moved to Chicago. There he hired a sturdily built young Swedish woman, Emma Nelson, to act as nurse to Sarah.

Sarah died in 1897, and six weeks before her death was so feeble she had to sign her name to her will with an X. The will disinherited all her relatives and left everything to her husband, William McClintock. Her half-brother, William Caswell, accused McClintock of "using poisonous drugs and intoxicating liquors to weaken her mind." He filed suit for his share of the estate, a suit that never got to court because McClintock settled with him for $100,000 out of a total valuation of $225,000—almost 50 percent of Sarah Hickling McClintock's estate. So, either there was some provable truth to the allegation that McClintock poisoned his wife, or he felt the estate would be seriously depleted by defending against the suit.[36]

Five years later, in 1902, fifty-three-year-old William McClintock married the woman who had been his wife's nurse: Emma Catherine Nelson, thirty-two, of St. Mary's, Kansas. On April 3, 1903, part of the Fatal Fortune's curse seemed to be broken with the birth of William Nelson McClintock, who was the first child born to any heir.

But it didn't take long for the curse to rear its ugly head again. On the afternoon of Friday, May 17, 1907, the McClintocks, four-year-old Billy, and an architect named William Krieg were driving in the McClintock automobile to look at a site the elder McClintock planned to build on. It was a time when not many people had cars, but McClintock was a real enthusiast and had owned them as soon as they were available. As they approached an intersection and made a turn, they found themselves in the oncoming path of a horse-drawn express wagon driven by young William Pennington. Confused by the automobile, Pennington kept trying to get his horse out of the way, but twice ended up pulling it in the same direction as the motor vehicle.

McClintock fought to steer his automobile away from the wagon, but Pennington's inability to control his horse caused a collision. One of the shafts from the wagon struck McClintock, and as it did so, Emma, sitting in the front with Billy, pushed her son to the floor—thus narrowly escaping being hit by a second shaft, which only grazed her shoulder. Krieg, the architect, suffered bruises but was not otherwise hurt.

William McClintock was taken to a nearby doctor's office, where he soon died of his injuries. An inquest found that the accident was unavoidable and exonerated Pennington of all blame, a decision that most likely reflects a distrust of the relatively new automobile. (In an interesting side note, all the witnesses at the inquest were male. Pennington, who could have been arrested for his actions, was allowed to testify, as was one of the victims, William Krieg. Yet Emma McClintock, who was able to give a very clear description of the accident to the newspaper and was on the scene for the entire event, was not included in the list of witnesses.)[37]

Because of William McClintock's shrewd investments in real estate and stocks, the Fatal Fortune, which had dwindled after the 1899 Caswell settlement to $125,000, was, in 1907, a robust estate valued at over a million dollars.[38] Emma now inherited one-third of this, as her husband had died intestate. Billy inherited the remaining two-thirds.

A scant two years later, in June 1909, Emma died very suddenly from what appeared to be heart disease, and six-year-old Billy was the beneficiary of the bulk of the fortune. As she was dying, Emma set up a trust fund to hold the money until Billy reached twenty-one, and appointed the Northern Trust as trustees. She designated two co-guardians for little Billy: Alexander F. Reichmann, a friend and lawyer employed by the Northern Trust; and her old school friend Julie Shepherd.[39]

Now young Billy had been struck down by the curse of the Fatal Fortune a mere eight months after turning twenty-one and inheriting it. Would the same misfortune afflict the Shepherds now that Darl was the latest heir?

Shepherd, a lawyer, had drawn up the will and knew very well what it contained: a discretionary annuity to Isabelle Pope and the remainder to himself. Yet, right after Billy's death, when he was asked about the terms, he told a newspaper reporter, Leola Allard-Day, that the money had been left mostly to charity, with some bequests to Mrs. Shepherd and her cousin Carl Sigfrid, a lawyer in Ouray, Colorado. Sigfrid, he explained, had been engaged to Mrs. McClintock before she married her husband in 1902. When Mr. McClintock died in 1907, Emma and Sigfrid again began thinking about marriage.[40] This is an interesting statement, inasmuch as the philandering Sigfrid was married at the time and also living with another woman while his wife was in California for her health. Supposedly, he had jilted Emma Nelson back in Kansas when they were first courting, and this was why she had moved to Chicago.[41]

To another reporter, Shepherd said that the majority of the estate would be used "for doing good in the world." Did this mean it was all willed to charity? Not exactly, Shepherd told him. It was Billy's wish to do good, and the will provided for expenditures for humanitarian purposes. The bulk of the estate would remain intact, but the interest would provide funds "for the good of humanity."[42] This patent lie was told at a time when Shepherd probably thought the terms of the will would never be made known to the public. (At the trial in June, the prosecuting attorney would sarcastically refer to "the charity" as the Shepherds themselves.)[43]

The same reporter asked Shepherd about Billy's impending marriage to Isabelle, and Darl—lying again—said that no date had been set. Would it have been soon if Billy had not died? the reporter wanted to know. "Probably Miss Pope thought so," was Shepherd's response. The reporter then asked whether Darl would have allowed them to get married before Billy's death. "Certainly not!" he answered vehemently. He would have thrown Isabelle out of the house if she had tried. What about the marriage license she got? "That was her business."[44]

Less than two weeks after Billy's funeral and burial beside his parents in Oak Woods Cemetery, the Shepherds left the Kenilworth house in the hands of a caretaker and traveled to Albuquerque, New Mexico, to visit with Mrs. Davidson. Two days before this, when they learned of a challenge to the will by some of Billy's cousins, Julie collapsed.[45]

Back in Chicago, Judge Harry Olson, chief justice of the municipal court, received a worrisome—and anonymous—letter. Olson's brother, the late Dr. Oscar Olson, had been the McClintock family physician for many years. The Olson boys had grown up in St. Mary's, Kansas, and knew Billy's mother and her family. Dr. Olson had at one time—like Carl Sigfrid—been engaged to marry the popular Emma Nelson McClintock. So Judge Olson was not about to ignore the message in the letter, despite the fact that he had no idea who had sent it:

> Find out what happened to Billy McClintock. He might have been poisoned.[46]

Chapter 2

The Grifters

They're nothing but a couple of lazy panhandlers.
—State's Attorney Robert Crowe

In 1924 William Darling Shepherd was an overweight, jowly, florid-faced man whose clothes always looked as if he had slept in them. His gait was described as "shambling,"[1] and he never exerted himself overmuch. He had large gaps in his front teeth, thick lips, and bulging eyes that were set too far apart, projecting the image of a none-too-bright, self-indulgent lump of a man.

Shepherd's wife, Julie, was a large woman about the same height as her husband (5'8"), although not as rotund as Darl, with a somewhat hard cast to her face and bright, shrewd eyes. It was difficult to see in her the young girl who had once been termed "the Belle of Salina, Kansas" at the turn of the century.[2]

Shepherd drifted, Forrest Gump-like, against the background of the exciting eras in which he lived. Another sort of man would have looked on it as adventurous and stimulating. But William Darling Shepherd was not that sort of man.

Drifted is the word most often used to refer to Shepherd, as he seems to have been primarily an aimless wanderer for much of his life. Back and forth between friends and relatives, from state to state, to whoever would provide him with food and shelter—this was the life led by William Shepherd. He himself once said he was "Mr. Nobody from Nowhere on the road to No Place," and it was probably the most accurate summing up of his character by anyone.[3]

Shepherd was born in Anderson, Indiana, on September 15, 1874, to William and Martha Harrison Shepherd. William Sr. taught speech (elocution) and physical education, and Martha read fortunes. They had five children: Alice, born in 1869; Preston, born in 1871; James Henry, who mostly went by Henry, born in 1872; William; and Gussie, born right after her father died in 1880. After the death of her husband, Martha gathered up the children and moved to the slums of Indianapolis. There she married a man named Presley Echols, who died soon after.[4]

A widow again, Martha Shepherd then married widower Benjamin F. Hayden, a man of many trades and all fairly, though not wildly, successful: he was a coal dealer, a real estate salesman, and a drugstore owner. Young William helped his stepfather in the drugstore, working there after school.[5]

When Willie, as he was called by his family, graduated from high school, he worked for a few months in the law office of Ferdinand Winter in Indianapolis. Around this time he began courting a high school classmate, Juliet Bohmie, daughter of a wealthy carriage manufacturer. One day while they were out riding, Willie was thrown from his horse and injured. Juliet took him to her home, which was close by—and there he stayed for five years, like the Man Who Came to Dinner.[6]

In the meantime, the Bohmies ran into financial difficulties when the carriage factory burned down. Willie stayed in the home to cheer up elderly Colonel Bohmie, whose wife had just died, while Juliet got a job in a department store. Although the two young people were semi-engaged, Juliet must have gotten a pretty good glimpse of what her life would be like married to an opportunistic slacker like Willie. She got engaged to, and eventually married, a man named John Lowry Ellis, who promptly threw Shepherd out of the Bohmie house.

In April 1898, Shepherd enlisted in the Army to fight in the Spanish-American War. He somehow attained the rank of sergeant, but never got out of his stateside training camp before being mustered out in November of that year. Still, that did not prevent Willie from regaling everyone he met with stories of his heroism in the Philippines. He told everyone that Theodore Roosevelt, at the request of a senator from Indiana, had given him a special lieutenant's commission. He also claimed he had been in the Battle of Spion Kop in the Boer War, where he got pushed off a cliff and stabbed in the shoulders. None of this was true. "He was the biggest liar in the company," his captain said later.[7]

One of Willie's friends was a songwriter named Paul Dreiser. Dreiser allegedly composed better when he was drunk, so one day Willie and some other boys got him royally liquored up and shut him up in his room. Dreiser, who was the brother of author Theodore Dreiser and later changed his name to Dresser to avoid that very connection, emerged from the room with what was eventually to be the state song of Indiana: "On the Banks of the Wabash."[8] Given Willie's propensity for making up stories, it is hard to know whether this one is true.

After the Army, Shepherd moved back to Indianapolis to live with his mother and stepfather. He attended night school at the Indianapolis School of Law for a while, but never graduated. Then he worked with his stepfather in the coal business for a few weeks, quit that (probably too much physical labor for him), and dabbled in the real estate part of Benjamin Hayden's enterprises.

Around the turn of the century, Shepherd went to Hickman, Nebraska, where his brother Preston had a decorating business. Willie worked there for a year, then drifted to Salina, Kansas, where he worked for a wholesale grocer as a receiving clerk, then as a stock clerk. This job lasted several months until he fell and hurt himself.[9] Possibly Willie was hoping that, as with his last fortuitous fall, someone like Juliet Bohmie would take him home; and that's just about what happened.

In Salina, Willie met the daughter of a prosperous barber who had set up one of his sons in a drugstore business. The daughter, Julia Marie Graf (known as Julie), was impressed with Shepherd's fake tales of heroism in the Spanish-American and Boer Wars and consented to marry the injured grocery clerk on what he said was his deathbed (he later claimed he thought he had a broken neck and was not long for this world).[10] As soon as the ceremony was performed, Willie made a miraculous recovery. Then he moved into partnership with Julie's brother, Otto, in the drugstore that had been purchased by Mr. Graf. Otto conveniently died in 1904, less than two years into the partnership, and Willie— who was now called Darl by his wife—ended up in sole possession of the drugstore.[11]

But Darl Shepherd could not remain financially stable for long, and soon difficulties arose. He had to sell the business in 1907, and he and Julie moved to Texas "to look for a location" (in his words), but they only stayed a few weeks.[12] During this time, the Shepherds learned of the tragic death of the wealthy William McClintock Sr., whose widow just happened to be an old classmate of Julie's from Bethany College in Lindsborg, Kansas.

Bethany College, situated not far down the road from Salina, Kansas, where the Grafs lived, opened its doors to its first class in 1881. It was originally an academy, or high school, before it amended its charter in 1886 to confer the baccalaureate degree. Its first four-year students graduated in 1891. Neither Julie Graf nor Emma Nelson was a four-year student and, although she was almost certainly there in some function, Julie Graf does not show up in Bethany's records at all. Her brother John graduated from the commercial department with a certificate in 1889, and Emma Nelson matriculated for two academic years (1885–1887) in the music department.[13]

The Shepherds decided to look up Emma Nelson McClintock and "help" her through the grieving process. Although there were occasional periods when they would stay in Indianapolis, they were—as Darl had been with the Bohmies—the Man Who Came to Dinner at the McClintock home. They simply never left.

Julie Graf Shepherd was about four years younger than her husband, born in Kansas on May 25, 1877, to Robert, a barber from Germany, and Anna Erickson Graf from Sweden. The Grafs had five children, of whom Julie was the second youngest: Edward John, Ulricka, Adolph Otto, Julia Marie, and Clara. They were also raising Anna's nephew Sigfred Peterson, who was nine years older than Julie.[14]

Peterson was born in Chicago to Swedish immigrants John Peterson, a tailor, and his wife Cecelia. He was given the name Charles Sigfred (or Sigfried) Peterson and some time before 1880 was sent to live with his maternal aunt and her family. (It is possible that his mother was either dead or too ill to care for him, as most men at that time did not raise children on their own.) By 1890 he had changed his name to Carl Sigfrid Peterson, and by 1900 he had dropped his original surname, for reasons unknown, thereafter referring to himself as Julie's brother or half-brother. Carl, like Julie, went to Bethany College to study for a while, although he was not a four-year student, and this is where he met Emma Nelson of St. Mary's, Kansas.[15]

Unlike her husband, Julie Shepherd was neither passive nor lacking in ambition. Physically imposing, masculine, and somewhat of a bully, she was given to energetic histrionics that probably made others afraid to oppose her. Possibly she saw Darl as someone whose life she could direct, while he saw someone who would give his life some stability. (An example of the difference in their temperaments occurred in an incident in 1923 when Darl was stopped by a police officer for driving thirty-three miles per hour through a business section. He accepted his fate calmly and was pleasant to the officer as the latter wrote up the ticket. But Julie angrily ripped into the policeman, nearly making the situation worse than it was.)[16]

If Julie thought Darl was going to be the breadwinner in the family, however, she was undoubtedly quickly disabused of that notion, and may have felt it was up to her to take charge of their united destiny. The drugstore business purchased by her father had failed, and the couple spent a few weeks drifting through Texas with no set purpose and no employment. It must have seemed a fortuitous event to find out that her old Bethany College chum, fellow Swede Emma McClintock, was now a wealthy widow.

When the McClintock case was prominent in the news, the Shepherds insisted that Emma had sent for them to comfort her in her time of mourning. But all who knew Emma—her servants, her friends, her physician—stated that Darl and Julie had shown up with their trunks and suitcases, uninvited, prepared to stay. They told Emma that the drugstore business in Kansas had failed, and they were "up against it."[17]

Julie soon overrode her more compliant friend Emma and took charge of the household. Darl did what he usually did: nothing. He worked for a chemical company in Chicago for a few weeks, then—as he put it—was "considering a proposition to go with the National Brush Company." But that got no further than "considering." He became a "gofer" for Emma McClintock, who gave him odd jobs now and then and used him as her chauffeur.[18]

At one point Julie approached Emma and asked if Emma could intervene with her lawyer, Alexander F. Reichmann, and get Darl a job in his law office. Reichmann, who had no use for either of the Shepherds and did not feel that Darl was competent enough to handle the kind of legal work that would need to be done, insulted him by offering him what was essentially an office boy's position. Darl refused it.[19]

Shepherd had spent quite a bit of time working in drugstores and even claimed to be a licensed pharmacist (he most likely was not). He enjoyed tinkering with chemicals and drugs (in high school he had taken a private course in chemistry from a tutor, on top of the one required for graduation), and had a laboratory set up in the McClintock home. Although he kept the lab locked up, several servants glimpsed it from time to time. They saw a Bunsen burner and 75–100 vials and bottles of various substances.[20] Shepherd once asked Emma for $400 to buy instruments to practice medicine, but she refused, commenting to one of her housemaids, "I can't see where we're traveling at" (meaning "I don't get the point of that").[21]

Julie's method of gaining control of the house on Calumet Avenue was to isolate Emma from any support system. She forbade the female servants to eat anywhere but the kitchen, whereas Emma, who enjoyed speaking Swedish with them, often had them sit at the table with her. When the phone rang, Julie hurried to answer it and would always tell the caller that Mrs. McClintock was not available—even if she was.[22]

Emma chafed under this tyranny, but could never bring herself to throw the Shepherds out. She told one servant—probably facetiously—to stop ironing Julie's clothes so that maybe she would leave. She complained to another about the rising costs of running the household and that the Shepherds never had any money. When she found out that Julie had restricted the servants to the kitchen, she told them she was sorry, but was apparently too cowed by her college classmate to countermand her orders.[23]

Emma was once visited by her late husband's niece, Mrs. Maud Walker, and Julie insulted the guest by commenting, loudly enough for her to hear, "I don't see why Emma takes in strangers."[24]

In 1908, when Billy was five, Emma McClintock wanted to adopt a little boy so her son could have a playmate. But the Shepherds objected to this so strongly that Emma abandoned the idea. At Christmastime that year, Julie's lawyer cousin, Carl Sigfrid, came for a visit and tried (unsuccessfully) to talk Emma into letting him manage the McClintock estate. Since he had once courted her, he probably thought he still had some power over her.[25]

During a land boom in Texas years earlier, Emma's husband William had purchased 581 acres in Chambers County and another 1,280 acres in nearby Galveston County. His plan was to develop a town and subdivide the land into city lots, but when the land boom failed, he abandoned his plan.[26] Darl Shepherd thought Emma should look to doing something with those properties and wanted to be put in charge of them. He convinced her to go down with him in early January 1909 to Bay View, Texas, near Galveston, where the Chambers County property was.

As the name implies, Bay View overlooked Galveston Bay, an inlet of the Gulf of Mexico. It was a breathtaking location, and Shepherd talked Emma into building a winter cottage there. She went back to Chicago, and he began superintending the project by hiring some of his relatives to work on it. The carpenter would be Jerome Matillo, whose first wife's brother had married one of Shepherd's sisters. The decorator/painter/paperhanger would be Darl's brother Preston, with another Shepherd relative as his assistant. They were all hired at the rate of $4 per day, the equivalent of $81 today.[27]

Shepherd ordered supplies from nearby companies in Bay View, Seabrook, Dickerson, Houston, and Galveston—paint, glass, wallpaper, livestock feed (he had decided they should raise some cattle), hardware, lumber, iron, furniture, and groceries for him and his crew—but stiffed the suppliers despite the $4,000 Emma had given him to pay them.[28]

During the course of the building, Jerome Matillo overheard Preston Shepherd ask his brother what he expected to get out of this project. "Don't you worry about Willie," Darl responded. "He'll come out with his pockets filled."[29]

While the cottage was being built, Darl found time to do some traveling with the Ringling Brothers Circus in Texas, possibly as a promoter. He had his fortune told (his own mother had always done this for a living) and the woman said to him, "You have a boy." "No, I don't," Shepherd said. "Yes, you have got a boy; there is standing between you and two women a big estate, and some day you are going to get that estate. The boy is going to die and then there is going to be a terrible explosion over it. But everything is going to be all right in the end." At any rate, this is what Shepherd later claimed the fortuneteller had said.[30]

That spring, Julie Shepherd went down to Bay View to join her husband. In late May, Emma, disturbed at getting bills from suppliers for unpaid goods and services, decided to go down there herself to see what was going on.[31] Soon after she arrived, she began to feel ill and worsened each day, despite the medicine being given her by Shepherd, the erstwhile druggist. He also drew up a will for her.[32]

Emma determined to go back to Chicago, stopping at Mudlavia Resort along the way ("There is that in my system which must be eliminated," she wrote her maid Stella Costigan, who was also a young widow with a child). She asked Jerome Matillo to take her to the train and, although she had refused to let Darl Shepherd accompany her to the station, he went along anyway. Emma told Matillo she was sorry she had ever started to build down in Bay View.[33]

Mudlavia was a popular mineral spa in Warren County, Indiana, near the Illinois border, that attracted clientele from all over the world. During Prohibition in the 1920s it was used as a retreat and hideout by Chicago mobsters. This is where Emma had met her husband: she and Judge Olson's mother had taken a trip there to alleviate the elderly woman's rheumatism; and William McClintock was there with his paralytic wife, Sarah. McClintock then hired Emma to be Sarah's nurse back in Chicago. (An ironic footnote to Mudlavia, from Emma McClintock's point of view, is that this was the place where Darl Shepherd's friend Paul Dresser debuted his famous song, "On the Banks of the Wabash" in 1899.)[34]

But Mudlavia's baths did Emma no good. She arrived in Chicago on June 3 sweating, jaundiced, and nauseated. The doctor was called, and when he saw her condition, he contacted her lawyer, Alexander Reichmann, so she could make a will. Reichmann had been a friend of Mr. McClintock from before his marriage to Emma and was concerned about the influence of the Shepherds in the home.

Emma's primary concern in making her will was to take care of Billy. She wanted to make her friend Julie Shepherd his guardian, pointedly omitting Julie's husband Darl, but Reichmann thought a better idea would be to make himself co-guardian with Mrs. Shepherd in a kind of checks and balances system.[35] Emma agreed, and also appointed the Northern Trust to be trustee of the estate until Billy reached age twenty-one. Despite the fact that she had signed the will drawn by Shepherd down in Texas, which made him executor of the estate and guardian of Billy, she signed this new one on June 4, 1909. What she had seen of Darl in Bay View probably made her leery of trusting him with the family funds.

Two days later, Emma drew up a holographic codicil to her will, making money bequests to various friends, relatives, and institutions. She left $5,000 to Julie Shepherd (but nothing to Darl).[36]

Why would Emma McClintock sign a will in Bay View, Texas, leaving Billy in the care of Darl Shepherd? And why, in her new will immediately preceding her death, would she leave him in the care of Julie Shepherd when she seems to have wished fervently that these two would go back where they came from? It is one of the mysteries of this case, especially since—according to them—two other longtime friends of Emma had been designated by her to raise Billy if she should die.

The answer probably lies in the personalities of Julie Shepherd and Emma McClintock. Emma comes across as non-confrontational, not even daring to brook Julie's orders to the servants, whom Emma was paying. Nor could she confront Darl Shepherd directly about his misuse of funds. (In fact, she gave him another $1,000 in Bay View to settle those outstanding accounts.[37]) While she could commiserate with her servants and express to them her desire to see the back of the Shepherds, she seems unable to have asserted herself in this matter.

Julie Shepherd, on the other hand, had a powerful, overbearing, and manipulative personality. Quite obviously, she brought up the subject of who would raise Billy, if not before Bay View, then certainly at that time, as Emma was so sick there. The meek—and physically weakened—Emma must have felt it was a good deal easier just to go along with Julie's wishes. If it had not been for the suspicious and foresightful Alexander Reichmann's creation of a joint guardianship, Julie would have been completely in charge of Billy's life from a legal standpoint.

Although this was never brought out in the *Chicago Tribune*, an article in the *Decatur [Illinois] Daily Review* quotes Dr. Krusemarck, Emma's attending physician, saying that she had originally asked him to be Billy's foster father. Krusemarck declined and suggested that she appoint her friend Julie.[38] It was odd that Emma should ask Krusemarck, as he was not her regular physician: Oscar Olson was, but was out of town at this time. It would have been more appropriate for her to express her wish that Oscar, rather than Dr. Krusemarck, take over the care of Billy.

This statement of Dr. Krusemarck also makes for a more random selection of Julie Shepherd as guardian, which Julie would certainly not have allowed. She would have made sure of her appointment before Emma left for Chicago and probably worked on her friend to that end. However, if the statement is true, it indicates that Julie was *not* Emma's first choice to raise Billy and that maybe she was trying to change whatever promises she might have made in Texas.

As Emma lay on her deathbed, hoping against hope that she would get well so she could take care of Billy herself, she indicated to Stella Costigan her exasperation with Darl Shepherd. What had he done with the $4,000 she sent him? She couldn't understand it, but the suppliers had not been paid. Also, she told the maid, Shepherd had incurred a separate debt of $500.[39]

In the meantime, notified by Alexander Reichmann about Emma's condition, Julie Shepherd rushed to Chicago to be at her friend's bedside and arrived on the morning of June 7. "My dear Emma!" she cried as she entered the bedroom and tried to wrap her arms around the dying woman. But Emma, who was struggling to breathe, pushed her away.[40]

At two o'clock that afternoon, Emma McClintock died of what Dr. Krusemarck assumed was pericarditis, as she had had a heart condition. She was two months shy of her thirty-ninth birthday.

Immediately after Emma died, Julie took a solitaire diamond ring from the dead woman's finger and put it on her own. "I'm saving it for Billy," she told the watching servants. But one of them later noticed the stone in a different setting and the old ring discarded in the trash.[41]

Down in Bay View, Darl Shepherd heard the news of Emma McClintock's death and prepared to head north. At the station, he was seen dancing on the platform as he waited for the train to Chicago. "What are you so happy about?" asked the stationmaster. "I just found out I'm to manage a wealthy estate," he replied, unaware that Emma had signed a new will a few days before. "I'm set for life!"[42]

When Shepherd arrived in Chicago and found out the terms of the new will, he was furious. He was also angry at not getting any kind of monetary inheritance, as his wife had. "I wish I had gotten here sooner," Julie told him. "If I had, the will would have been different."[43]

Emma McClintock was buried in what Judge Harry Olson thought to be unseemly haste. He had been shocked when he saw her blackened, swollen corpse, and thought there should be an autopsy. But exactly forty-eight hours later Emma was buried next to her husband in Chicago's Oak Woods Cemetery. The reason the Shepherds gave for the hurry-up funeral was that the presiding minister had to go out of town. Judge Olson was so upset over the whole thing that he refused to be a pallbearer.[44]

The cottage in Bay View was abandoned, unfinished, after Emma's death. The bills for goods and services that were to have been paid by the $5,000 she had given to Shepherd for that purpose ($4,000 before he left for Texas and $1,000 when she went down there in May) were now paid from the estate—an estate that had been considerably depleted over the two years since Mr. McClintock's death and the arrival of the Shepherds.[45]

Back on Calumet Avenue, Darl and Julie went about raising six-year-old Billy, who was frail and often sick as a child. The guardians got $1,000 a month from the McClintock Trust to take care of him, plus expense money. They insisted he call them Mother and Father, and he seems to have treated them as such. Darl Shepherd whipped the boy with a belt when he misbehaved, and Billy would run to one of the female servants pleading, "Save me! Save me!"[46] However, this kind of punishment was standard fare in families back then and does not seem to have been more abusive than the norm.

Billy's illnesses were attributed to nervous attacks, which came about when he got overly excited. These episodes seem to have arisen after his father's death, and possibly were the result of his having witnessed it and being almost injured in that accident. As an example of the frequency of Billy's problems, Dr. Oscar Olson submitted his bill to Emma's estate for having attended the little boy fifteen times between December 25, 1908, and March 5, 1909.[47]

During Emma McClintock's lifetime, Darl Shepherd had tried to alienate her from Alexander Reichmann, her attorney and the manager of her estate. He told her and her friends that Reichmann was cheating her by telling her the Texas properties were not worth very much and that she should sell them, and he insinuated that Reichmann was helping himself to the estate. Now that Reichmann was co-guardian of Billy, the Shepherds tried to diminish his control over their young ward. They told the shy little boy that Reichmann was the boogeyman and not to be trusted, that he would try to kidnap him in his automobile.[48]

One day, at Reichmann's insistence, Billy had dinner with the lawyer and his family, who had a little girl slightly older than Billy and one who was younger. The boy seemed fearful during the whole meal, and when Reichmann proposed an automobile ride (a novelty in the first decade of the twentieth century), Billy ran crying from the house.[49]

The Cook County Probate Court records are full of filings back and forth between the Shepherds and Reichmann over the raising of Billy. The Calumet Avenue neighborhood was changing in that the "red light" district was getting closer to it, and Reichmann did not think this was a good neighborhood for raising a little boy. He proposed that the trust buy a home in the northern suburbs, closer to Reichmann's home, where he could have more contact with his ward. The Shepherds refused to move.[50] (The Calumet Avenue house is today much better located, near McCormick Place and directly eight miles south of Wrigley Field, off Lake Shore Drive.)

Right after the death of Billy's mother, the Shepherds wanted to take him out West, to the Alaskan-Yukon-Pacific Exposition in Seattle, being held in the summer of 1909. But Reichmann, backed by two physicians, said this trip would not be good for Billy's fragile health because it would cause him to get too excited, thereby triggering an attack. The lawyer thought maybe a calmer trip to New York State's Adirondack or Catskill Mountains would be better.

However, the Shepherds took Billy out West anyway—not to the Seattle Exposition, but to Colorado to consult with Julie's lawyer cousin, Carl Sigfrid, to learn how to wrest control of the estate and Billy away from Reichmann and the Northern Trust. That this happened within a month or two of Emma's death is indicative of their determination. Reichmann found out they had gone and, furious, insisted they have a conference with him. But they went directly to Indianapolis, instead telling Reichmann that Darl's mother had an accident and broke some ribs. This was a lie, as they admitted later. Their real purpose in the Indianapolis trip was to consult further with Sigfrid, who was visiting there.[51]

Who was this Carl Sigfrid, who appears throughout this saga at critical moments? After his time at Bethany College, he had gone to Ann Arbor Law School (today the University of Michigan), graduated in 1890, and then settled in the little town of Ouray in the southwestern corner of Colorado, near Telluride, where he specialized in the odd combination of representing mining claims and prostitutes. While he was at Bethany he met the woman who would later be his wife: Elice Svenson, a music major like Emma Nelson. (Quite possibly, this is the woman he jilted Emma for.)[52]

By 1900, Carl and Elice had two daughters, but that year she took the girls and moved to California, ostensibly for her health (needing to be at a lower altitude than the mountains of Colorado) and until the girls finished their education. Possibly other things were behind this drastic move, however, because as soon as Elice was out of town, Carl moved in with his stenographer, divorcee Minnie Bugby, and her fourteen-year-old son.[53]

When Elice returned in 1916, having lived in California apart from her husband since 1900, she found him living with yet another woman, Erin Reisor Gilbert, a divorcee ten years his junior, who presented herself as his wife. Elice began divorce proceedings, charging adultery, and Carl countered with charges of abandonment. The whole thing was very messy and both were found guilty of the respective charges. However, Elice was granted alimony.[54]

People in Ouray County claimed that Sigfrid had a woman in every town where he practiced law, which covered considerable ground.[55] So his possible romancing of the newly widowed Emma McClintock right after her husband died would not have been out of the question, even though he was still legally married to Elice.

At one time a Chicago businessman, Charles H. Nix, hired Sigfrid to help him with some mining interests he had purchased in the Ouray area. But the relationship eventually soured and Sigfrid filed a defamation-of-character suit against Nix. When Nix found out about it, he scoffed, "Character, character, that man has no character; it isn't safe for him to be at large; he isn't safe anywhere, even in a sewer, without a muzzle on him." Sigfrid's response was, "When that old fossil is shoveling coal below, I'll be singing in the Celestial Choir."[56]

Sigfrid seems to have had some of the same storytelling tendencies as his cousin Julie's husband, Darl Shepherd: he told the people of Ouray that he had been a defense attorney for Richard Loeb in the Leopold-Loeb case in Chicago in 1924, but his name does not appear in any of the official records or accounts of the case. He claimed to be a relative of Loeb and that he had been summoned back to Chicago by the family to help the young man with his legal difficulties.[57] However, as Loeb's relatives were from Germany (mostly Jewish, although his mother was Catholic) and Sigfrid's were Lutherans from Sweden, it seems highly unlikely that he was related to them. The family that called him back to Chicago for legal aid would have been the Shepherds.

Despite his failings as a husband, Sigfrid was a successful attorney, known for his sharp mind and his sharp tongue. By 1901 he and his law partner, Lyman I. Henry, were able to have a large edifice constructed for their offices: the Hayden Building, named for nearby Mt. Hayden. Today, it is one of Ouray's most beautiful historic buildings. Later, Sigfrid was permanently retained by the Denver & Rio Grande Railroad to represent their interests.

An Ouray resident at the time Sigfrid lived there claimed that the lawyer had a tunnel built in his newly constructed Hayden Building to connect its cellar with a house across the alley. Sigfrid then amassed facts about Ouray County residents from a series of informants who used the tunnel to convey information.[58]

After the incident in which Julie and Darl took Billy to Colorado without permission, then lied about having to go to Indianapolis, Alexander Reichmann took them back to court and asked that Julie Shepherd be stripped of her guardianship. Reichmann wanted to raise the boy himself. But Julie promised to do a better job and agreed to allow the estate to buy the house in Kenilworth that Reichmann had picked out because it was close to his own home. Its purchase price of $65,000 is equivalent to $1.25 million today.[59]

Kenilworth, Illinois, which today ranks among the top of America's wealthiest suburbs, was incorporated in 1896 by Joseph Sears as a planned community for the privileged, who would form a network of "congenial, child-focused families." Sears placed restrictions on lot sizes, construction, and inhabitants. Daniel Burnham, the chief architect of the sumptuous Chicago Columbian Exposition, designed Sears's own house. In 1896 the population of Kenilworth was 300; today it is 2,500: the city is 96 percent white, with a median income of $200,000 and with the average home costing $1.3 million.[60]

Darl Shepherd continued his wheeling and dealing during Billy's growing-up period. In 1910 he told the census taker that he was a real estate salesman.[61] In 1911 he owned and ran something called the People's Show Card Concern, which may have been for booking carnivals and other exhibitions. This lasted fourteen months, after which he traded the business for a farm in Kansas that he put in his wife's name.[62]

After that, Shepherd sold lands in the South on commission and set himself up in various offices in downtown Chicago. In 1916 he went to work in the law office of Boos and Stoll, then was admitted to the bar in Illinois in 1917. Boos and Stoll dissolved their partnership and Shepherd became Robert H. Stoll's new partner, but this only lasted a short while.[63]

Darl seems to have spent a lot of his time eating in Chicago's many restaurants. One of the places he frequented was a saloon and seafood restaurant at 5066 Broadway, run by Louis Sbarbaro. One day in 1917 Sbarbaro was opening oysters, a popular menu fare of the time, and Shepherd asked him to point out the part of the oyster that contained the poison.

"What?" Sbarbaro asked incredulously.
"I heard that oysters have poison in them. Where, exactly, is it located?" Shepherd repeated.
"What the hell do you do for a living?" Sbarbaro asked him.
"I'm the guardian over a millionaire boy out near Evanston."
"You've got a soft job, then," Sbarbaro commented.
"Someday I'll have a barrel of money," Shepherd bragged.[64]

In 1919 Darl contracted an intestinal problem. His friend and physician, Dr. Oscar Olson (brother of Judge Harry), had him admitted to American Hospital for it and also for the removal of his tonsils and the correction of a nasal problem. While there, Darl met an attractive young nurse, twenty-four-year-old Estelle Gehling, and began an affair with her that would last for several years, until at least 1924. One of his frequent laments in his ardent letters to her was, "If Billy marries, I'll be out in the cold."[65]

When the romance between Billy and Isabelle got more serious, the Shepherds began to worry. "I don't know what will become of us if Billy marries," Darl told a friend.[66]

Julie attempted to control Billy through emotional blackmail. She demanded constant reassurance that he cared for her and Darl. When he was at Dartmouth and not writing home often enough, she had their pastor, Rev. Carl Naumann of St. Paul's Lutheran Church in Evanston, write to Billy and scold him for writing so much to Isabelle but neglecting his "dear mother." So Billy wrote home.[67]

One summer Billy, Isabelle, and the Shepherds took a trip to State Line, Wisconsin. Julie saw Billy kiss Isabelle, and from that point on became cold and distant. As they ate their lunch, Billy commented on her aloofness: "Come back to earth. You look as if you were in China."

"I wish I were," was Julie's peevish response. "You always said that when you were twenty-one you would take us abroad with you on a trip around the world. But I never expect to go now. I never expect to go."[68]

Julie made Billy promise he would not get engaged before he turned twenty-one, and he agreed. But he and Isabelle got secretly engaged two years before that, in 1922, when they were nineteen. Billy purchased a ring from Peacock's Jewelers in Chicago and couldn't wait for Isabelle to begin wearing it so all the world would know of their commitment.[69]

The secret engagement took its toll on both Billy and Isabelle, especially since they were apart at this time. During a normal engagement, they would both have refrained from going out with other people, but Billy did not want Isabelle to be deprived of socializing. He thought she should go out with friends, but Isabelle didn't always want to do this. Still, when she did go out with a young man, usually in a group, Billy felt threatened. He seemed to think she should walk a fine line between going out and not actually being accompanied by anyone. It was a frustrating situation, as revealed in Isabelle's letters.[70] From November 1923:

> Now when someone comes along who gives me a good time you find a little fault. You know you can trust me, and what if people do doubt that I'm engaged to you? We don't want them to know it until we announce it. Sweetheart, you are mistaken about my going with him all the time, but why sit home when I get a good chance to go out? ... You know yourself that boys don't take girls out when they realize the girl uses them only as an accommodation. You say you want me to go out and have a good time.... Now, Harry Keighly gives me a good time and as few others ask me out, why should I refuse his invitation? ... Now, dear, if our engagement was announced everything would be different, but we can't act as if it were some times but not other times.

From January 1924:

> For years I have been in a most difficult position, engaged and yet not engaged, while you were not hampered that way at all.... Please don't worry about Harry, Sweetheart. I'm not going to go with him too much. He is not a [Northwestern] man now and his taking me out doesn't mean a thing. After all, dear, our engagement isn't announced, you know, and isn't even known to our own families really. You know, honey, that I wouldn't go out with any one else if you were home.

With Billy away at Dartmouth, Isabelle often spent time with the Shepherds at the Kenilworth house. They seemed to have accepted her as their future daughter-in-law, and she began to view them as another set of parents. But Julie sometimes acted strangely. Once, after dinner, she drove Isabelle home in Billy's car. She told her to pretend that she, Julie, was Billy. Then Julie began to talk to her as a sweetheart would. It gave Isabelle the creeps. At another time Julie teased the young girl that she should get her hair bobbed (a controversial fad of the 1920s) because it would look very attractive on her, despite the fact that Billy hated the look and was adamant that Isabelle not cut off her beautiful hair.[71]

Although on the surface the Shepherds were kind to Isabelle, behind the scenes Julie was playing her control games with the servants. She presented Isabelle as a bossy tyrant and told them, "That pest is trying to marry Billy." She led the servants to believe that their lives would be a living hell if that ever happened and that Isabelle was only after Billy's money. (She seems to have succeeded with at least one servant, the cook, who tore up a picture of Isabelle and spit on it.) Julie was heard to moan on occasion, "What will become of us if Billy marries her?" and once stamped her foot and declared, "This marriage shall never take place." When Billy was sick in November and typhoid had not yet been diagnosed, the doctor placed a quarantine sign on the door of the residence, thinking his patient had the flu. "Now we can keep her out," Julie said smugly.[72]

Louis Kles, the houseman and chauffeur, said he was told to spy on the two young people whenever Billy came home from college, and then report to the Shepherds what they said and did. Kles never did this, however, as he didn't consider himself a "stool pigeon."[73]

After Billy left Dartmouth, two women (unnamed, but almost certainly Ruby Peel and Mildred Davidson) went to see Judge Charles S. Cutting, the jurist who presided over the legal proceedings regarding the McClintock trust and the guardianship. They wanted Cutting to tell Billy that by getting married, he was not showing his appreciation to Julie! The judge told them it was none of his business and that Billy was an adult and could make his own decisions. The women claimed that Julie did not know they were there, but it is more probable that she sent them on this absurd mission.[74] Did she think Billy would remain single forever out of a sense of loyalty to her?

The Shepherds must have felt that things were quickly spiraling out of their control with Billy's coming of age and his newfound sense of independence. In a letter to Isabelle in May, a month after his twenty-first birthday, he reflects this self-confidence and also some displeasure with his guardians. It sounds as if he intended to break ties with them after his marriage to Isabelle:

> I haven't heard from the folks in weeks. I suppose I have committed some frightful boner or something, but really I can't bother to find out until they write. I really think they will both be happier if they have their little farm or home in Florida and don't bother about me. I wonder what they will say when I announce my revised plans for the care of what properties I have. I don't care much, for I am at last sure of myself, and, well, I have heard that people are better off without too much sentiment.[75]

When Billy came home from Dartmouth in June 1924, to take over his estate and attend business school close to home, he had two other goals: to announce his formal engagement to Isabelle, with a prospective wedding date of June 1925, and to sell the Kenilworth home. He would buy a home in Chicago or in Florida for the Shepherds, he told Isabelle in a letter, but the house on Melrose Avenue was too big and, at $700 a month in 1924 (equivalent to over $7,500 today), it cost too much to run.[76]

Billy listed the Kenilworth house with a broker without consulting the Shepherds, and when they found out, they were vehement in their opposition. When prospective buyers came to look at the house, Julie told them it was not for sale.[77]

Then Billy formally announced his engagement to Isabelle Pope on July 1, with another bombshell: instead of a wedding in June, they had moved it up to February 22. When a neighbor commented to Darl Shepherd, "I understand Billy is to be married," Darl's response was, "He thinks he is."[78]

In spite of their distress at this new turn of events, the Shepherds must have congratulated themselves for their foresight in getting Billy to sign his will that April. In fact, the idea for the will in the first place was probably theirs and not Billy's at all. Even though Darl Shepherd would later claim that Billy thought of it on his own and had even sent him a memorandum from Dartmouth as to what provisions he wanted (a memorandum never seen by anyone), the words of Assistant State's Attorney George Gorman at the trial in June 1925 ring true: "What does a boy of twenty-one think of? Certainly not of death—he is prodigal of life and time at that age, and death is farthest from his thoughts."[79]

Chapter 3

The Avenging Fury and the Confidence Man

It's an easy matter to obtain typhoid germs. They're easier to get than pistols and you don't have to pay for them.
— Dr. David J. Davis, University of Illinois professor
of microbiology, 1925

The drama of the Millionaire Orphan was played out against the backdrop of what was arguably Chicago's most exciting era: the Jazz Age. Post-war cynicism and a booming economy had evolved into a hedonistic free-for-all across the country, an attitude that would later be celebrated in Cole Porter's 1934 classic song "Anything Goes." It could have been an anthem for the 1920s.

Probably the most drastic change from the pre-war years was in the young people. Staid and proper young ladies gave way to flappers who wore short dresses, went to men's barber shops to get their hair bobbed, and took off their girdles to dance. They attended "petting parties" and necked with young men in the backs of automobiles. They smoked in public. And they drank.[1]

The case of twenty-one-year-old Robert Allen Preston, a Northwestern University student and the son of wealthy Oak Park parents, epitomized "modern flaming youth" to the people of Chicago. In April 1925, as the McClintock inquest was underway,

Preston's body was found in Lake Michigan with a bullet in his head, the result of suicide.

Preston left behind three very detailed and somewhat shocking diaries that told of his debaucheries and his unsuccessful attempts to live with diabetes. In defiance of his condition, he indulged himself in every aspect of life: he stayed up late, drank a lot, picked up girls, got speeding tickets (and was sometimes taken to jail for them), ate whatever he wanted, and lied constantly to his parents about where he was going and what he was doing. ("I feel somehow that I am a goner," he wrote in his diary in February. "O, when I can't say but I believe within the next year. So, hell, I'm going to have a good time. No [insulin] shots.")

Bob Preston's last diary entry for 1924 is a sad one:

> Well, so this diary is ended. I don't know how long I will keep it or how often I will read it. I have seen some happy but more sad times. It is more the reading of a tragedy than a comedy. I would like to have started it sooner for then it would have included when I first started to go bad. My first kiss, my first mug [necking], my first drink, my first carouse, my first overdose of insulin ... and 101 other things.... When you get to the end of your rope tie a knot and hang yourself.

Preston was determined to live hard and then die, since he did not want to cope with his diabetes. Although his diaries reveal a myriad of excesses that were almost certainly unusual in their freneticism, parents and preachers looked at his life as a prime example of what was wrong with the young during the 1920s, ruined by gin and jazz. Preston's words and his suicide became the stuff of a cautionary tale for his generation, and parents were warned to pay more attention to what their offspring were up to—in effect, "Be your children's diaries." (Bob Preston's father insisted that he was unaware of his son's drinking, but the diaries present many parental confrontations at three o'clock in the morning, so he couldn't have been truly ignorant.)[2]

Prohibition, in effect in the 1920s, was more honored in its breach than in its observance, and the illegality only made the whole process more titillating for all ages. College fraternities had no difficulty getting booze to share with their members and their old grads up for the weekend football game. Certainly Bob Preston's diaries show that alcohol was easily available. One judge admitted that he drank more in his own chambers during Prohibition than he had done anywhere else before that.[3] Speakeasies provided patrons with secret, private clubs, and the ever-present possibility of a police raid made the experience a heady one for normally law-abiding citizens.

But in the spring and summer of 1924, a year before the McClintock inquest and Robert Preston's suicide, a more sober face had been put on the "anything goes" philosophy with the arrest of two wealthy Chicago teenagers for the thrill killing of a fourteen-year-old boy. Nathan Leopold and Richard Loeb, both nineteen, were not only wealthy (Loeb's father was a vice president of Sears, Roebuck), but geniuses as well. They had already finished college and were in graduate school in 1924, Leopold at the University of Chicago and Loeb at the University of Michigan. Leopold's IQ was an unbelievable 210; Loeb's was 160.[4]

Both boys, neighbors and inseparable friends, were disciples of the philosopher Friedrich Nietzsche and his concept of the superman who is above the law. They decided to try out the theory and prove to themselves that they were truly exempt from the restrictions that bind the common people, so they selected a victim at random: fourteen-year-old Bobby Franks, also a neighbor. They lured him into their rented car, bludgeoned him with a chisel, stripped off his clothes, and stuffed his body into a culvert. Then they contacted the boy's parents and attempted to get $10,000 to return their son alive.

The kidnapping ploy failed when a worker happened upon the body in the culvert before the money could be dropped off. Various clues left at the scene led authorities to Dickie and Babe, as they were known to their friends, and left Chicagoans shocked beyond belief. In a surprising move, instead of insisting on a prolonged trial and hoping for an acquittal, the boys pleaded guilty. The only issue left to decide was their punishment. Enter Clarence Darrow, the most famous attorney of the day (and probably of any day). His impassioned speech before Judge Caverly to spare the boys' lives is a legal classic.

Darrow's opponent was Illinois State's Attorney Robert E. Crowe, who wanted the death penalty imposed on these dangerous young men, whose motiveless crime (not for lust or for money or for vengeance, but for the hell of it) was unfathomable to most people. But Darrow's argument about the barbarity of executing two misguided teenagers was so persuasive that Judge Caverly instead issued sentences of life plus ninety-nine years for each.

A more usual kind of violence that formed the pattern of everyday life in Chicago in the 1920s was the activity of mobsters, flourishing in the era of Prohibition. That November, while Billy McClintock was coming down with typhoid fever, mobster Dion O'Banion was gunned down in his own florist shop. Fellow gang member Bugs Moran figured he knew exactly who had ordered the hit and proceeded, over the next several months, to knock off three of the notorious Genna brothers one by one.[5]

The Genna boys were bitter rivals of the O'Banion mob, so it was a natural assumption for Moran to make. But he was wrong. The killing was orchestrated by an up-and-coming member of Johnny Torrio's gang trying to gain a stronger foothold in Chicago's crime scene: Al Capone. The jockeying for position and tit-for-tat retaliations after the O'Banion murder would culminate in the St. Valentine's Day Massacre in 1929.[6]

One man who had seen his share of the criminal element in Chicago was Judge Harry Olson, chief justice of the municipal court. A former prosecutor in the district attorney's office, Olson had been elected to the newly created position of chief justice in 1906 and would hold it for twenty-four years.[7]

Olson was born in Chicago in 1867 of hardworking Swedish immigrants Olof and Clara Olson. Olof, a stonemason, had brought his family to America after the birth of their first son, Oscar, at the end of the Civil War. Oscar, who would go on to become a physician, was four years older than his brother Harry, who was, in turn, four years older than the youngest boy, William.

After helping to build the Chicago Water Tower, Olof moved his family to St. Mary's, Kansas, where the Olsons became acquainted with the Nelsons and their little girl, Emma. In 1880 Olof was killed when a wagonload of stone crushed him, and Harry went to work for a country lawyer to help support the family.

Before he had even graduated from Washburn College in Topeka, Harry was a teacher and then a principal in the same St. Mary's public school where young Emma Nelson was enrolled. In 1891, he graduated from the law school that would eventually become Northwestern University School of Law and settled in Chicago with his wife Bernice. Emma, before her marriage to William McClintock, boarded there with them.

Harry Olson, an extremely able and skilled lawyer, was nothing if not impassioned. He championed the rights of those less fortunate, and when he became obsessed with an idea, he was like a terrier with a rat. It could never be said of him that he was passive and uninvolved, as was the case with William Darling Shepherd. Once, when leaving City Hall, Olson came across a group of men having a fistfight in the corridor. Four were flailing away at each other and a fifth lay bleeding on the floor. He tried to get them to stop, but one of them hit him and knocked him down. The judge entered the fray ("to defend myself," he later said) and yelled for help. The responding police sergeant quite naturally assumed Olson was one of the fighters and grabbed him, while the real culprits ran away. Harry got a black eye for his trouble and was so incensed at the policeman that he swore he would have him arrested.[8]

Nor was Olson afraid to tackle Chicago's political icon, the powerful and corrupt "Big Bill" Thompson, who reigned as mayor for twelve years. The chief justice ran against him in 1915 and again in 1919, but lost in the latter primary by 40,000 votes.[9]

So when Harry Olson got the anonymous letter about the possible poisoning of Billy McClintock, he characteristically jumped into action, immediately applying for an exhumation order and an autopsy. Because of his standing in the legal community, he was granted this. The exhumation of Billy's body from its resting place in Oak Woods Cemetery took place on Christmas Eve.

"Who's doing that? Who ordered it?" was Darl Shepherd's reaction to the exhumation when he was contacted in Albuquerque by a reporter from the Chicago Tribune. It was the first he had heard of it.[10]

Judge Olson insisted he had good reasons for the exhumation. He had still not forgotten his disquiet over Billy's mother's death and his suspicions that the Shepherds were up to no good with their ward. A few hours after Billy's death, Darl Shepherd's former law partner Robert Stoll came to the judge's office to tell him about it. Olson felt Stoll was trying to discern whether the judge would cause any trouble over it. "Well, Bill McClintock's dead," Stoll told Olson, and the judge thought sarcastically to himself, "At last."

Olson told Stoll to handle the will fight if one should arise, and the attorney asked about Billy's relatives. Olson knew very well who they were, but needed to buy himself time to get his case together to order an inquest done. He gave Stoll the names of three deceased cousins in Kansas. At the funeral, Stoll was telling everyone that Billy didn't have a relative in the world— he had obviously hunted these three down and found they had already died, but didn't bother investigating further.[11] (This incident, so soon after Billy's death, indicates that perhaps there *was* no anonymous letter about Billy's being poisoned.)

Harry Olson's sister-in-law, the doctor's widow, was told by Shepherd that she couldn't go to Billy's funeral because he had died of a contagious disease and the health department forbade attendance by anyone other than the Shepherds. At that time she asked Shepherd if the Kansas relatives had been notified, and he told her Billy didn't have any. Mrs. Olson set him straight on that (not being privy to the judge's secret plan) and gave him their names. Then she phoned the health department and discovered that no such quarantine had been placed on Billy's funeral, nor was there an epidemic of any sort.[12]

Shepherd seems to have wanted to get Billy in the ground as quickly as possible with no witnesses and no suggestions of an autopsy. Not only did he try to prevent Dr. Olson's widow from attending, but he never told Alexander Reichmann, Billy's co-guardian, that the boy had died. Reichmann found out from someone else and said that, after that, he was followed by detectives hired by Shepherd.[13]

Readers of the *Chicago Tribune* awoke on Christmas morning to find the front page of their newspaper filled, not with messages of peace and good will, but with stories of heartbreak and tragedy. The night before, in Hobart, Oklahoma, a holiday pageant in a one-room schoolhouse resulted in lighted candles on a Christmas tree setting fire to the small building. Thirty-two people, mostly children, were killed when they could not get out the one doorway. Almost forty others were seriously injured, many of whom were expected to die.[14]

Then there was the report of Billy McClintock's exhumation because of suspicions about his death. An autopsy would test for poison. Isabelle Pope, still in deep mourning, was shocked at this turn of events and could not believe the insinuations that Darl Shepherd—who most stood to gain from Billy's death—was in any way responsible. Despite their differences in the past, she stood up for him.[15]

Shepherd, however, was not so generous. He was busy putting a positive spin on everything that looked bad for him, and what most people focused on was his refusal to let the young couple get married. Calling Isabelle "mercenary" for wanting to marry Billy on his deathbed, he said that he was actually involved in a "friendly plot" with Billy because the sick young man wanted to wait until he was better.[16] (But Isabelle had been the one who put off the original wedding date until February, while Billy had wanted to get married as soon as possible. Moreover, the Popes were quite well off, as were most of the young people in Isabelle's set, so Shepherd's labeling of her as a gold-digger was unfair and untrue.)

Shepherd had an answer for everything. Was there any rupture between Billy and the Shepherds? On the contrary, Darl said, the young man's last words were, "I love you, Mother dear." Why had they left so fast after his death? Mrs. Shepherd had had a nervous breakdown and wanted to go to Albuquerque for her health. What about the statements Darl had made to various people that he didn't know what would become of Julie and himself after Billy married? He denied ever saying such a thing. He and Mrs. Shepherd were glad that Billy had found such a nice young lady as Isabelle Pope, and they had plenty in the bank to support themselves (this, despite bank records that showed that Shepherd had an average balance of under a dollar over the previous several years and never more than a few hundred dollars at any one time).

On the advice of his attorney, his former partner Robert Stoll, Shepherd got on a train for Chicago on Christmas night to answer questions at the state's attorney's office. Julie would stay behind, supposedly too ill to travel at that time. At about the same time the California Limited sped through Kansas City, Missouri, carrying Shepherd back to Illinois, a doctor at the famous Kellogg Sanitarium in Battle Creek, Michigan, came forward with startling news: when he (the doctor) worked in Chicago, Shepherd had frequently consulted him about the cultivation of typhoid germs.[17]

From 1917 to 1920, Dr. Frank T. Breidigan, a bacteriologist, had been in charge of the Illinois Research Laboratory on North Wabash Avenue. He first met William D. Shepherd when the latter came in with Dr. Oscar Olson to have a blood test taken on Billy. Later, Shepherd came periodically to see Dr. Olson for his own medical problems.

Dr. Olson introduced Shepherd to Dr. Breidigan as a pharmacist and, indeed, Shepherd showed a great familiarity with the reagents on the lab shelves. He was very curious about certain kinds of germs, particularly tuberculosis and typhoid, Breidigan said, and in all, he came to the lab about six or eight times to ask questions and look under the microscope. Sometimes he stayed for fifteen minutes, sometimes for as long as a couple of hours, picking the bacteriologist's brain about TB and typhoid germs.

Stung by Breidigan's unexpected accusation, Shepherd lashed out at what he called "my traducers," particularly Judge Olson, who could expect a lawsuit when all was said and done.[18] He denied that he had ever studied chemistry (he had, in fact, taken a special course in chemistry from a private tutor, as well as the one offered by the high school),[19] denied that he had ever studied bacteriology, and denied that he was a licensed pharmacist.

The latter was probably literally true, because the pursuit of this kind of certification would have taken too much energy and dedication for Darl Shepherd. Still, he had bragged to many people—including a reporter right after Billy's death—about being licensed.[20] And he had worked as a druggist in Indianapolis with his stepfather and in Salina, Kansas, with his brother-in-law. So, even without the certification, he had quite a bit of pharmaceutical knowledge. Then there were those vials and bottles in his laboratory at home, and his practice of dispensing pills and tonics to those around him who were ailing. Shepherd wasn't exactly the ignorant layperson that the defense would later try to present him as.

Shepherd admitted talking to Dr. Breidigan and looking under a microscope at some TB cultures. But, he insisted, he had never seen a typhoid germ in his life. Further, he said, this whole thing was a plot cooked up by Judge Olson and the McClintock cousins, who were challenging Billy's will. When Shepherd arrived from Albuquerque on December 27, he vowed to file multiple lawsuits against everyone who tried to besmirch his name.[21]

Shepherd also declared that he would break the "hoodoo" curse of the Fatal Fortune by separating it into several funds to be used "for the betterment of mankind" after the deaths of Darl and Julie. He would set up a trust fund for Isabelle Pope to make sure that she got the $8,000 annuity. In the will, he had conveniently made this annuity discretionary and not mandatory.[22]

By New Year's Eve, the autopsy on Billy and subsequent tests had been completed. There were no metal or vegetable poisons in the body, and the cause of death was determined to be a very strong, but normal, case of typhoid fever. There were several cases of typhoid that November, most of them the result of eating raw oysters at the "Gold Coast" (the wealthy towns on the north shore of Lake Michigan) homes and restaurants. These oysters, declared Health Commissioner Dr. Herman Bundesen, could have come from beds in the East that were very close to the Passaic Valley sewer, which every day put out 100 million gallons of sewage.[23]

The incubation period for typhoid fever is about eighteen days, and this timing would coincide with Billy's consumption of raw oysters at the Windermere House on November 3. Besides, Dr. Bundesen declared, it was not easy to get typhoid germs unless someone were connected with a legitimate hospital, doctor, or medical school. (He would later change his tune about this.)

With the verdict about the poisons in, and the matter seemingly at rest now, Isabelle Pope, whose grief had been exacerbated by the thought that Billy's guardians might have murdered him, went to Los Angeles with her Aunt Belle after the first of the year.[24]

But Judge Harry Olson, self-styled "avenging fury" and "attorney for the dead," would not let the matter go. State's Attorney Robert Crowe, who had just finished his successful prosecution of teenage murderers Nathan Leopold and Richard Loeb that September—successful even though he didn't get the death penalty for them—was reluctant to proceed with the Shepherd case. He didn't think the evidence warranted it. So Judge Olson brought up the matter of the deaths of his brother Dr. Oscar Olson in 1921 and of Billy's mother in 1909. He felt Darl Shepherd was responsible for these as well.[25]

Dr. Oscar Olson, Harry's older brother, had been appointed by the court to be Billy's physician. Prior to marrying his wife Louise, Dr. Olson had been engaged to Emma Nelson McClintock and was a longtime friend of the family. But gradually, after Emma's death, the Shepherds kept Billy away from Dr. Olson and replaced him with Dr. Rufus B. Stolp, who had no prior connection with the Nelsons or the McClintocks. Although Dr. Olson and Darl Shepherd had been "pals" at one time, by 1921 the doctor was doing his best to undermine the Shepherds' control of Billy. He had decided to advise Billy that, as soon as the young man turned twenty-one, he should take charge of his own affairs and not let the Shepherds have any control of his estate.

Dr. Olson and Darl Shepherd had been estranged for several years when the doctor came down with ptomaine poisoning. He was on the mend when Billy came to visit him, and Dr. Olson then advised Billy—as he had in the past—to be wary of the

Shepherds. The day after that, the Shepherds, who had not been to Dr. Olson's home in six years, came to visit the convalescing patient with another friend, retired Chicago publisher Thomas A. Newman. They brought a big basket of fruit, and at one point Darl Shepherd asked to speak with Dr. Olson alone. Julie Shepherd, Thomas Newman, and Louise Olson left the room.

Dr. Olson later told Louise that Shepherd just wanted to tell him about some lands in Texas that had produced a gusher, hoping he could get the doctor to invest in them. But that night Dr. Olson became so sick that he died the next day. It was a shock to his family because he had been declared out of danger, and his condition at the time didn't seem to warrant such a drastic change in his health.

Judge Olson now presented this as evidence that Shepherd possibly poisoned his brother, and he ordered an exhumation. At the same time, he voiced his suspicions about what really killed Emma McClintock. As a result of these allegations, the coroner's jury merely declared a recess instead of issuing a verdict of "no criminal action" in the death of William Nelson McClintock.

Back in Albuquerque after his trip to Chicago, Darl Shepherd reacted to the new charges as "the ravings of a disordered mind" and presented his side of the story. He claimed he had visited his "old pal" Dr. Olson several times a week, and that the fruit was in an unopened basket brought by Thomas Newman, not the Shepherds. As to the statement that Dr. Olson didn't trust the Shepherds and told Billy this, Darl declared it a "pure fabrication."[26]

As a show of support for the Shepherds and their fight to clear their names, the pastor of their church, Rev. Carl Naumann, sent them a telegram to say that Darl Shepherd had been elected a vice president of the congregation. Naumann's telegram read as follows:

We express heartiest approval of your message of faith and good will [the Shepherds had sent their own statement to the church's annual meeting]. We have never had the slightest doubt of your own faith and consecration to the Lord and Master, and feel assured He will answer our prayers that your vindication will be complete in every sense.[27]

Rev. Carl Naumann, fifty, seems to have dedicated his entire ministry to being at the beck and call of the Shepherds. He shows up everywhere: after Emma McClintock died, Naumann made a special trip to Bay View to clear the cottage of the Shepherds' things, including a box containing the medicines Darl dispensed so freely.[28] He wrote to Billy at Dartmouth to scold him for neglecting Julie. He was constantly in the home when Billy was dying. He presided at the funeral. He claimed it was his suggestion that the Shepherds go to Albuquerque so they would not have to face Christmas in their house without Billy. When the press began hounding the caretaker in charge of the Kenilworth house in the Shepherds' absence, she called Naumann to handle them.[29]

Was Naumann a co-conspirator, if conspiracy there was, or an innocent dupe? Judge Olson called him "the false face of decency on this hideous, monstrous deed."[30] But judging from his record and his pictures in the newspaper, he seems to have been a guileless, naive, well-meaning busybody who firmly believed that his friends and parishioners, Darl and Julie Shepherd, had nothing to do with the death of their ward.

While Darl Shepherd and Judge Olson were trading insults in the newspapers, and the coroner's jury was looking for evidence that would connect Shepherd to any of these deaths, former nurse Estelle Gehling emerged to recount her affair with William Darling Shepherd and gave his love letters to the jury. What was most damning in them was not his cheating on his wife, but his constant lament about being thrown out on the street when Billy eventually married.[31]

As he had with Dr. Breidigan, Shepherd admitted knowing Miss Gehling, but that was all. He couldn't remember that he had sent any letters that might be termed "love letters." He and Dr. Olson had gone to a few parties with Miss Gehling and another woman, but these were entirely innocent occasions, ignoring the fact that two middle-aged men out with young women not their wives could never be viewed as entirely innocent. Miss Gehling began coming to him for money, so he broke it off, he said. Once she even sent a woman friend, "Blossom" Taylor, to threaten him.[32]

Shepherd insinuated that Estelle Gehling was trying to blackmail him, but that he had no money to pay her off, so he just refused to deal with her (as if this could deter a blackmailer). Shepherd claimed that his wife was not reading the newspapers those days, so knew nothing about either Miss Gehling's story or the inquiry into Billy's death.[33]

Estelle Gehling was philosophical about Shepherd's denial:

> He was a silly old man, looking for sympathy—you know how a man gets sometimes when he is getting fat and tired of his wife.... He's just trying to cover up his affair.[34]

But soon enough everyone would know of it. Summoned again from Albuquerque to appear before the coroner's inquest in February, Shepherd—despite his oft-proclaimed eagerness to tell his story and clear his name—declined to testify, practically running from the courtroom after invoking his Fifth Amendment rights.[35] So he missed the reading in court of his letters to Estelle Gehling, although the newspapers jumped at the opportunity to present this latest scandal to their readers.

Because of Shepherd's constant references to her in his letters as his "darling sunshine," the newspapers dubbed Miss Gehling "the Sunshine Girl." Darl Shepherd had claimed he didn't think he had written anything that could be termed a "love letter" to her, but there was no doubt in anyone's mind once they were read:[36]

June 1, 1920

Sweet Darling,

Started to write May instead of June. Forgot that this is the bride's month. Wonder if I can name a bride for next June? Hope so, I'm sure.... I am very anxious to see you, dear. Seems an age since that most happy Friday eve. I certainly had a dandy time and was so happy.... Don't forget, dear, I love you, my sunshine, and I am so happy in your love. Take care of yourself, sweetheart. Lots of love and kisses from your own.

Darl

Later, this one:

Oct. 1, 1924

Dear Girl:

Things have come along like a cyclone since seeing you at noon. Can't go into all the details, as Mrs. S. is waiting for me in the outer office. Merely say that at about 1:30 a deal came to a head and broke me flat, absolutely bankrupt and no hope for the future. I think I will drift away from it all. Just Nobody from Nowhere on the road to No place.... I am wild about you and would give my life rather than

harm you, yet I took all of your dear, sweet self, deluding myself that
I would find a way, as I have always done before. The money that I
sent Saturday—and I hope that death may take me if I am not telling
the truth when I say it—was about the last of my cash in hand, and
now that is gone and it is doing no good.... Life means nothing to
me now. I do not know which way to turn nor what I shall do. I
could fight back if only the money were involved—the thing that I
can't fight is that I win the one thing in the world that I crave, your
love and respect, and then I lost all again.

Signed, "D"

Asked later about what this "deal" was that fell through,
Shepherd claimed there was none, that he had made it up.[37] But
the timing of this last letter, with its reference to financial problems, is interesting: a month before Billy fell ill. And the recency
of the letter made a liar out of him when he said he couldn't
remember writing love letters to Miss Gehling. The tenor of this
last one indicates that Shepherd was probably paying her for
sexual favors ("I took all of your dear sweet self," but then
couldn't send more money).

The following day another bomb was dropped on the inquest
by the indefatigable Judge Olson, whose function here seemed to
be as orchestrator of evidence to be presented (although he kept
forgetting that he was not in charge and had a tendency to blurt
out rulings on attorneys' objections):[38] he had come up with another
witness who would connect Shepherd with an interest in typhoid
germs. Dr. George E. Fosberg testified that he had answered questions for Shepherd in the spring of 1924, the result of a referral
by a mutual acquaintance with an "easy bookkeeping" system.[39]

Fosberg said Shepherd paid him $50 over two sessions (about
$550 in today's money) for telling him where to get the germs,
the effects of certain poisons, and whether poison would show
up in an autopsy if it were given to the victim in oil. (Shepherd
had often given Billy castor oil for his "bowel problems.")

The cover story Shepherd told Dr. Fosberg was that he had a
relative, a young man, who had died under suspicious circumstances, and he wanted to know whether certain poisons or germs
could be detected. One of these was bichloride of mercury, but
when Fosberg told Shepherd it could be detected many years
after death, Darl did not pursue the discussion. Over the two
conversations he held with Fosberg, he narrowed his focus to
one poison (prussic acid) and typhoid.

By this point Darl Shepherd's interests in court were being represented by another attorney, Edwin Hedrick, as Robert Stoll did not have much criminal defense experience. Stoll stayed on as an assistant to Hedrick, and Shepherd began showing up in court, probably at their insistence; it wouldn't look good if he stayed away.

Hedrick proved to be as feisty as Judge Olson. The two exchanged hostilities on the second day of testimony until Judge Olson took exception to one statement: "I'll protect myself against such remarks," he declared, moving toward Hedrick with his fists up. But the judge's son, Sanford, who worked in his father's law office, came between the two and prevented the fight. Hedrick fired a parting shot at Judge Olson: "You dirty rat!" whereupon the coroner rebuked the defense attorney and called a recess so everyone could cool off.[40]

Shepherd's defense team had hired the John Jones Detective Agency to investigate some of the witnesses and allegations. The primary method of this agency, whether by direction from the defense attorneys or on their own, was to bully, blackmail, and beat witnesses. One of their operatives was told to go to Dr. Fosberg's office and lure him away with a story of a sick girl. Fosberg got suspicious, called Judge Olson, and soon a policeman was on the scene. The operative admitted that it was a ruse, but claimed he had no idea what his employers intended to do with Fosberg. The chief of police thought they probably wanted to make him unavailable to testify, but Judge Olson was convinced they intended to bribe him to change his story.[41]

Likewise, Louise Olson, widow of Dr. Oscar, got a phone call telling her that her brother-in-law, Judge Olson, wanted to see her in his office. Not trusting this information, she phoned the judge herself and discovered he had sent no such message. Mrs. Olson also claimed she had been "menaced" since testifying about Shepherd's activities in her home right before her husband died.[42]

Lawrence Clody, foreman of the inquest jury, received several vaguely threatening phone calls, and then his florist shop was bombed. Later, Judge Olson himself was threatened with great bodily injury if he didn't lay off his investigation in the Shepherd case.[43]

By the end of the month, Judge Olson (who referred to the Shepherds as "parasites living on the McClintock estate")[44] had come up with two more surprise witnesses: John P. Marchand and Earl Clark, former employees of the National University of Sciences in Chicago. It was Earl Clark who sought out Judge Olson because he was bothered by an incident involving Marchand, and then Marchand was dragged in, somewhat unwillingly.

Clark told Olson that Marchand had talked about a letter that would be worth a lot of money if he could get hold of it. Marchand had been reading in the newspaper about the McClintock inquest, recognized Shepherd, and exclaimed to the three men with him, "I know that guy!" He said that the letter he referred to was written by William Darling Shepherd inquiring about signing up for some courses in bacteriology. Marchand tried to get Clark to steal the letter for him so he could blackmail Shepherd, and this is what sent Clark to Olson. The other two men, both chiropractors, backed Clark's story.[45]

John P. Marchand's real name was Patrick John McMahon, a World War I veteran and railroad worker who had been blackballed for his union activities. The reason he had changed his name was so that he could get a job, although he told the court that his wife didn't like his given name.[46] Marchand was something of a wise guy on the stand, so he probably meant this sarcastically.

In 1924, Marchand was a soliciting agent for the National University of Sciences, whose director, Dr. Charles C. Faiman, had given him Shepherd's letter of inquiry and told him to visit the lawyer's office with a view to signing him up for courses. But, Faiman warned Marchand, he should proceed cautiously: this could be someone trying to investigate the school.

Marchand went to the address in the letter, met with Shepherd during lunchtime, and found out that he was interested in bacteriology from a defense attorney's point of view: how germs could be cultivated, propagated, introduced into a victim's body, and whether they could be detected at autopsy. He also wanted information about purchasing laboratory equipment. Rather than press the issue of enrollment, however, Marchand, who smelled "undercover agent," instead told Shepherd he would have to see Dr. Faiman to get this information. He then reported back to Faiman and left the damning letter with his boss.[47]

On the day Marchand was to testify at the inquest, he was put (probably by Judge Olson) in the back of the jury box to see if Shepherd showed any reaction. Marchand claimed that Darl never took his eyes off him.[48]

On cross-examination, Marchand, who answered most· questions with one of his own, claimed he would never have tried to blackmail Shepherd with the letter. "If I thought the letter was valuable, would I be blabbering around there about it to strangers? I was just passing the bull around."[49]

In order to corroborate Marchand's testimony and provide another link in the chain of evidence against Darl Shepherd, the court would need to hear from the director of the National University of Sciences: Dr. Charles C. Faiman.

Charles Andrew Claire Faiman was born on December 16, 1899, in Hopkins, Minnesota, near Minneapolis. He graduated from Hopkins High School in June 1917 and spent the following fall semester at the University of Minnesota's College of Liberal Arts before dropping out.[50] Although he would later claim otherwise, this one semester was the entire extent of Faiman's higher education at a legitimate school.

In the early 1920s, Faiman matriculated at a correspondence "diploma mill" school based in Oskaloosa, Iowa, that was legally or illegally using the name of the old Oskaloosa College that had become Drake University around the turn of the century. Drake relocated to Des Moines, but J. W. McLennan either purchased the original Oskaloosa College charter or merely appropriated its name for the operation he ran out of a downtown business office.

Rumors abounded in Oskaloosa about the legitimacy of the degrees McLennan was conferring, so an enterprising reporter set up a trap. He got enough evidence to enable McLennan to be prosecuted by the federal government for using the mails to defraud. However, before anything could come of it, both McLennan and his wife committed suicide, giving as a reason their financial inability to defend themselves against what they termed "this unjust charge."[51]

Charles Faiman claimed to have attended Oskaloosa College for nine months, receiving a degree called PhB (bachelor of philosophy),[52] and it may have been this experience that gave him the idea for his National University of Sciences.

Faiman was a genius. Top medical men said so.[53] Creative, insightful, and with an almost intuitive knowledge of medicine and bacteriology, he nonetheless preferred the heady thrill of earning his living by scamming people. In fact, he put more thought and energy into these enterprises than most people put into their regular jobs; and, while many of those with big schemes and big dreams often fail to realize anything from them, Faiman was successful in whatever he put his hand to, legal or not.

Faiman's legitimate jobs included assisting at autopsies at the University of Minnesota and also working in the university's pathology lab. He was employed by Dr. Charles E. Fischer, the head of Fischer Laboratories in Chicago, from October 1920 to January 1922, except for a three-week period in 1921 when he told his employer he was going to St. Louis to "buy a diploma." When he came back, he added another degree to his resume: an MD from the St. Louis College of Physicians and Surgeons. In the 1920 census, Faiman, only three years out of high school, listed himself as a physician, and he would do so on every official document for the rest of his life.[54]

During his years in Minneapolis, when he was still in his teens, Faiman's scam was to contract to buy, often with no money or just a few hundred dollars down, small delicatessens, then use these to enter into large purchase orders with suppliers. He would then sell these goods at auction and not pay the wholesalers. Nor would he go through with the purchase of the delis.[55]

Charles Faiman was so glib, bright, and confident that he came across as older than he really was. In fact, he usually added five years to his age when asked for it.[56] He was dapper in appearance, had a receding hairline, and wore a mustache, all of which contributed to the illusion.

In 1921, Faiman found his greatest opportunity of all. For $250 he bought, at a sheriff's auction, a failing school called the American College of Pathology and Bacteriology and renamed it the National University of Sciences. It had no accreditation or standing even before his purchase and consisted of a single brownstone house at 2923 South Michigan Avenue, next to a millinery shop.[57]

As the original school had been founded in 1907, Faiman's pamphlet for 1923 misleadingly announced its "16th successful year." National University also offered courses in theology, law, and midwifery, as well as those in the regular sciences. Although a handful of students attended lectures and labs in the traditional way (taught by Faiman and another instructor), in the short time Faiman owned the school, he issued approximately 700 degrees to "students" who had never set foot on the campus but had merely sent in the fee.[58]

Faiman's promotional pamphlet for the school boasted a faculty laden with degrees from prestigious schools: Harvard, Purdue, Columbia, Yale, and a boatload of foreign universities. None of this was true. Even the janitor had a degree: DB—for doctor of bacteriology—because he kept the place germ-free![59]

Diploma mills may seem like an amusing artifact from a benighted past, but in today's cyberworld they thrive more than ever. An investigation between July 2003 and February 2004 revealed that "at least 28 senior-level federal employees in eight agencies have bogus college degrees, including three managers at the office that oversees nuclear weapons safety." One employee admitted he had paid $5,000 for a master's degree, but never had to do anything for it. Who footed the bill for these fake degrees? The taxpayers.[60]

Even today, only four states outlaw such degrees.[61] One of them is Illinois, probably as a result of legislative proposals drafted immediately after Faiman's school was exposed in the newspapers.[62] But at the time of the Shepherd case, there were no such restrictions, so Faiman's school—strictly speaking—was not illegal. Once, an official at the Illinois State Department of Education and Registration asked him why he didn't choose to run a proper school instead of a diploma mill, and Faiman answered, "Why should I make my school a real one? I can make a lot more money running it the way I do than I could if I hired regular instructors."[63]

Charles Faiman had a real love of the sciences, especially pathology and bacteriology. This is one of the reasons he actually taught some legitimate courses (the other reason was to present a respectable front for inspection) and why he had, as one detractor reluctantly admitted, as up-to-date a laboratory as any licensed hospital had.[64] To get vials of bacteria for his students and for his own study, he went to the Department of Health and talked a clerk into giving them to him. One clerk was a girl he flirted with before he got married, Alvira Armstrong, and the other was a young man listed as one of the board members of the National University: Winfield Scott Hoerger, nephew of a former Chicago alderman.[65]

Not content to rest on his laurels collecting money for issuing fake degrees, Faiman used his "university" in other ways. He claimed that, as part of the school, he had a teaching hospital with actual patients—although, in reality, he had neither. This was because, during Prohibition, hospitals could be issued alcohol for patients. When Faiman got his monthly alcohol issue of ten to thirty gallons, he sold it out of various hotel rooms around Chicago. He did the same with narcotics, usually selling to middlemen who would then distribute to others. One of his hotel-room clients was currently serving a term in Fort Leavenworth for selling drugs. But Faiman himself never got caught.[66]

There were rumors that Faiman was performing abortions at his school and that one woman had died on the operating table, but nobody ever came forward to substantiate this.[67] However, it was most likely true, and he was not the only medical man in the Shepherd case to be accused of this. The sexually liberated 1920s produced many inconvenient pregnancies, and both licensed and unlicensed physicians performed abortions. It was a lucrative business, and rarely prosecuted unless the woman died during it. A poll of middle-class women during the 1920s indicated that 10–20 percent of them had had abortions.[68]

So when Charles Faiman read the letter of inquiry from William Darling Shepherd in the fall of 1923 about taking classes in bacteriology, he was suspicious. He told his sales employee, John Marchand, to follow up on it, but to be cautious and not give away too much. Marchand did, but thought Shepherd might be an undercover agent, so referred him to Faiman.

A week after Marchand's visit, Shepherd went to National University to talk to Faiman.[69] Faiman showed him around the facilities, which were legitimate, and Shepherd wanted to know if he would be able to buy his own microscopes and other lab equipment. Two days after that, Shepherd returned for a lesson in bacteria cultures: the differences among them (tuberculosis, typhus, diphtheria, etc.) and how they were kept alive. Faiman told him that, although TB germs were very slow, typhoid bacteria could grow to a full culture in eighteen hours. He had three vials of typhoid germs he had just gotten from the health department—paratyphoid A, paratyphoid B, and regular typhoid—and gave these to Shepherd, at the latter's request, after showing him how to keep them alive. (Paratyphoid by itself was not fatal, but if mixed with regular typhoid the result was even more virulent than typhoid alone.)

Shepherd did not contact Faiman again until April or May 1924, right around Billy McClintock's twenty-first birthday. At that time he set up a meeting in the Palmer House, Chicago's best-known hotel, and indicated an interest in bacteriology from a criminal standpoint: had bacteria ever been used to kill anyone, and could it be detected?

It is not known how Faiman responded to this, but by 1924 there were two famous cases involving homicide by bacteria: the suspected murder of several members of the Swope household by Dr. Bennett Clark Hyde in 1909 (Kansas City, Missouri) and the murder of his in-laws by Dr. Arthur Warren Waite in 1916 in New York City. Both killers used typhoid, but Waite also resorted to more traditional poisons and even ground glass to make sure the deed was done. Waite confessed, but—after three trials—Hyde got a hung jury.[70]

Shepherd came right out and asked Faiman for the best, most efficient way of infecting someone with typhoid germs, and was told that they would be colorless, odorless, and tasteless in water, and would not trigger the stomach's release of acid to destroy them. Shepherd said he still had the germs Faiman had given him, and wanted to know how to transfer them to the water.

Faiman informed Shepherd that typhoid was not always suspected at first when a patient got sick because the symptoms were the same as for flu, so the infected person was not usually given the antidote until it was too late. Solid food, which would not hurt a flu sufferer, was bad for a typhoid victim, and the worst thing of all was a "physic" or laxative. Food and laxatives could tear the intestinal lining and cause hemorrhaging.

It must be asked at this point exactly what Faiman, the shrewd operator, thought was going on. He can hardly have been an innocent naif, blithely sharing—without receiving any fee—information of a deadly nature in secret meetings in various hotels instead of on his campus. (They had met at the Palmer House, the Sherman House, the grillroom at the Atlantic Hotel, and the lobby of the Morrison Hotel.) Even before he heard of Shepherd's wealthy ward, he had to have suspected early on that the lawyer had a plan to do away with someone by using the typhoid germs.

At one point Shepherd went to the school and asked Faiman if he could look through the files. Faiman claimed he allowed this, and that Shepherd then found the inquiry letter he had written (signed with a fake name but using his correct office address), took it, and gave the scientist $50 for it. After this, Faiman seems to have taken the gloves off and shed the cloak of innocence—if, in fact, he had worn it at all during his meetings with Shepherd. He told Shepherd they should come to some kind of "arrangement," with the insinuation being "after Billy dies."

Shepherd, in his stupidity and greed, evidently thought he could get the germs and the bacteriology lessons from Faiman and not have to pay him anything. Possibly he selected Faiman on purpose and thought that if it ever came to "he said/he said," people would believe the upstanding Shepherd and not the con man Faiman. At any rate, when Faiman suggested a quarter of a million dollars as his piece of the pie, Shepherd merely laughed at him. Eventually, they compromised on $100,000, to be paid when the estate was settled after Billy's death. Shepherd would come to regret not taking better care of Faiman.

That Faiman honestly believed he would be coming into $100,000 can be seen in his letter to an architect in mid-January 1925 for plans for a medical school, which would accommodate 200 students and have ten classrooms and laboratories, an auditorium, and a library, among other things. The projected cost for the school was $100,000. Maybe Faiman intended to go legitimate after all.[71]

Toward the end, according to Faiman, both men got bolder and more specific in their conversations, although they were still careful not to speak overtly about murder for fear of being overheard. They referred to Billy as "the cub," and Shepherd— as he had with everyone—expressed to Faiman his concern about being left out in the cold if Billy got married. He insinuated that he was only looking out for his and his wife's interests in getting rid of "the cub." (A man later came forward to say he had seen the two together in one of the hotels and overheard Faiman tell Shepherd to "watch out for the cub," at which point Shepherd assured him, "Oh, don't you worry about that. I've handled this sort of thing before."[72] But, as this witness was never brought in to testify, it may be that his story was not believable.)

When Billy got sick, Shepherd and Faiman met in the lobby of the Morrison Hotel, not even staying long enough to sit down. Shepherd seemed "a little disturbed" at this meeting as he told Faiman about Billy's illness. When Faiman asked about treatment, Shepherd said he had given the boy a cathartic. Neither man mentioned the vaccine, which would have been helpful at the onset of the disease.

After Billy's death, Shepherd called Faiman and told him he was going south for a few weeks, probably so Faiman wouldn't panic and do something rash. When Judge Olson's accusations hit the newsstands and Shepherd had to come back early, Faiman got nervous. But Shepherd told him not to worry, that everything would turn out all right.

However, Marchand's recognition of William Darling Shepherd in the newspaper and his subsequent entry into the case interested the state's attorney's office in questioning Faiman to back up Marchand's story. Faiman at that time denied knowing about any such letter and denied knowing Shepherd, but did acknowledge that some vials of typhoid bacteria had been stolen from his lab in the fall of 1923.[73]

The prosecutors were stumped. One guy, Marchand, claimed he went to Shepherd's office at Faiman's request, while the other guy, Faiman, said he didn't know anything about it. How to reconcile this? Recognizing Marchand/McMahon as a hotheaded Irishman, they put him in the same room with his former boss and settled down to wait. It didn't take long. First, angry words could be heard coming from the room ("Liar! Liar!"), and then a thumping sound. When they went in, Faiman was on the floor begging for mercy, and Marchand was standing over him, insisting he tell the truth.[74]

Faiman then changed his story. He acknowledged knowing Shepherd ("I could never forget those nephritic eyes") and said that the lawyer had taken a weeklong course in bacteriology at National University. Faiman claimed he never asked for any fee from him because he thought he might be a county agent checking on the school. Then, after Shepherd left one time, Faiman found three vials of germs missing.[75]

It was about two in the morning when Faiman's questioning began, yet whenever the door of the interrogation room was opened, he would wave happily at the reporters camped out in the hall. He never lost his natty appearance.[76]

Eventually, Faiman implicated himself in the scheme more and more. He finally admitted that he had *given* Shepherd the typhoid germs, and that it was understood that Shepherd would not use them until after Billy had signed his will. Faiman claimed it was his own idea that the will include a gift to the fiancee to throw off suspicion and prevent her from complaining.[77]

With Faiman's testimony, State's Attorney Robert Crowe finally lost his lukewarm attitude toward the case and got an arrest warrant for William Darling Shepherd. When Shepherd was brought in the night after Faiman's questioning, he denied knowing his accomplice. Thinking the same technique might work with these two that worked with Marchand and Faiman, they put Shepherd and the scientist in the same room together. Faiman, indignant, accused Shepherd of concocting the entire plot to kill Billy, but Darl never lost his cool: "I never saw you before," he insisted calmly.[78] It would seem that a more natural reaction to a false accusation of murder by a stranger would be an angry and forceful denial.

Faiman had not only connected William Shepherd to the murder of Billy McClintock, he had also incriminated himself as an accomplice. From this point on, the nexus of the case hinged around this story and whether Faiman could be believed. That he was a consummate confidence man cannot be denied. But what possible motive would he have had to make up the story? He put himself in legal jeopardy, as he was neither promised nor given any immunity; was arrested along with Shepherd; and had his beloved school (although it was mostly a scam, Faiman was very proud of its legitimate aspects) exposed to ridicule and possible closure. Even before trial began, he was lamenting the loss of students as a result of the charges against him and resented National University's being dubbed "a mill of quacks": "Now my school will be ruined and my pupils gone," he said angrily to reporters in a rare show of temper.[79]

Faiman was put in the Briggs House, a Chicago hotel, instead of jail, probably to ensure his eventual cooperation at trial as the key witness against Shepherd. There he was able to order hotel meals and have his wife bring books to him. (One Chicago resident, a lawyer, was so incensed at the expense involved in paying for Faiman to stay at the Briggs House that he filed a lawsuit based on his standing as a taxpayer.[80])

In actuality, Faiman had been admitted to $100,000 bail, but it was "posted" without funds by two police sergeants, who put him in the hotel as their personal prisoner. This was Crowe's idea so the state could retain custody of Faiman, and every morning they had to present him to Judge Thomas J. Lynch. Faiman had a great time at the Briggs, and one night was seen dancing and enjoying girls at the Silver Slipper until the wee hours.[81]

But despite his somewhat privileged status, Faiman had no attorney. When he was offered one, he turned it down—a decision that was not in his best interests.[82]

As a result of Faiman's statements, the Chicago City Council drafted and passed the Chicago Germ Ordinance, which made it unlawful for anyone "other than a public official to keep, sell, barter, or trade in cultures having pathogenic germs" unless the individual got an annual license for $1. Hospitals were exempt from the licensing fee. Even though applicants had to state their qualifications (education, experience, etc.) for getting the germs, it is hard to see how the ordinance could prevent someone like Faiman—who manufactured his qualifications—from paying the $1 and getting the germs. Even the recordkeeping requirement could be gotten around by a smooth con man in a pre-computer era.[83]

Because of his unresolved legal difficulties, Faiman resigned his post as president of National University and appointed Earl Livingstone, a former post office clerk, in his place.[84]

As the state prepared its case against William Darling Shepherd, prosecuting attorneys had to wonder: would a jury believe a man like Charles Faiman?

Chapter 4

Hippodrome

*They talk about me not being on the legitimate. Why, lady, nobody's
on the legit when it comes down to cases; you know that.*
    —Al Capone to reporter Genevieve Forbes Herrick, 1929

The year 1925 started out ominously for the nation. In January,
sixteen-year-old San Francisco girl Dorothy Ellingson was told
by her mother that she could not go to a jazz party that night.
So Dorothy shot her mother, stepped over the body, and went
to the party as planned. When she was arrested, the young girl
showed no remorse over what she had done. Her attorneys used
the unique defense of insanity by jazz: the music had taken over
her mind and made her crazy. The jury didn't buy it.[1]

In that same month a Kentucky cave explorer, Floyd Collins, was
trapped for nearly three weeks under a seventy-five-pound rock
while the nation followed the progress of the rescue. A young, pre-
Spirit-of-St.-Louis Charles Lindbergh was hired to fly photographs
of the death struggle to Chicago newspapers. People brought their
families from all over the country to camp out at the site and watch
the proceedings, while ambitious entrepreneurs took advantage
of this to set up food and souvenir stands. As the various rescue
groups bickered on the top over who had prior rights and what
recovery method to use, Collins starved to death down below.[2]

The story of Floyd Collins was America's biggest media event after World War I and would remain at the top until Lindbergh's crossing of the Atlantic in 1927. Enormous headlines in the nation's newspapers from back then would lead modern readers to assume that the plight of Floyd Collins was a local one. The cave explorer's dilemma, the drama of the rescue, and the subsequent tragedy bound Americans together in a common story as nothing else had done since the war. It *was* a local concern, after all: everybody cared about what was happening to Floyd Collins.

In March the worst tornado in U.S. history killed 695 people in Missouri, Illinois, and Indiana, wiping out several towns before it was spent. The Tri-State Tornado still ranks at the top of the list in terms of destruction and lives lost.[3]

The *Chicago Tribune* had become militant in its criticism of what it saw as the top evils of the day—autos, guns, and moonshine—and in each paper published the current total on a "hands of death" clock. By July 1, 1925, the figures were 387 deaths attributed to autos, 206 to guns, and 130 to moonshine.[4]

Because Billy's death had attained such a high profile and it was known that he had eaten raw oysters at a restaurant, the state health commissioner issued an order that raw oysters no longer be served in eating establishments.[5]

On March 13 in Chicago, with the confession of Charles Faiman, State's Attorney Robert Crowe ordered the arrest of William D. Shepherd in a sort of "midnight raid," possibly to catch Shepherd off guard and scare him into an admission of guilt. But someone obviously leaked it, because when police arrived, both Darl and Julie were up and dressed and the ubiquitous Rev. Carl Naumann was there also, as was Shepherd's former law partner, Robert Stoll. A large bulldog "greeted" the arresting officers, but was quickly calmed by Shepherd.

As Darl was taken away, Julie "stormed and sobbed," appealed to God to vindicate her husband, and in general acted "with the dramatic fire of a [Sarah] Bernhardt: 'It's exactly like a crucifixion!'" she wailed. She called her husband's prosecution "a frame-up conceived wickedly out of pure imagination, a sensational story on the top of a slippery, wicked, lying foundation."[6]

As for Shepherd himself, he seemed unfazed by the circumstances. On the way to jail, he smoked cigarettes in an amber holder, chatting nonchalantly with the officers about fishing and about "his" land in Bay View, Texas.[7]

At the Cook County Jail, Shepherd went to the head of the line of twenty-three other arrestees awaiting processing. Because of his status, it was assumed that the usual procedure of fumigating suspects and their clothing was not necessary for him, so he was quickly escorted to cell number 13 (known as "the clean cell"), which adjoined those shared the previous summer by the notorious teenage killers Nathan Leopold and Richard Loeb.[8] At some point he was taken out and put into the same room with Charles Faiman to see if he would crack. He didn't.

Back in his cell, Shepherd stretched out on his bunk and quickly fell asleep. No tossing and turning for him. In fact, he told reporters later, jail was not bad at all:

> I slept like a log last night. And my appetite is great. I've eaten three big meals since I've been here. My cell is clean and the bed might be a lot worse.[9]

Shepherd's placement in cell number 13, the "clean cell," was somewhat ironic, as it had last been inhabited by a consummate con artist, Leo Koretz. Koretz had swindled many people for millions of dollars by selling them stock in a Panamanian oil company—a company that existed only in his imagination. He was sentenced to one to ten years in Joliet, a sentence that was "commuted" by his death there from diabetes in 1925.[10] The young diabetic Robert Allen Preston, who would commit suicide that April, wrote this entry in his journal:

> Jan. 9—Friday—Koretz the swindler died today of diabetes in Joliet pen. God! the poor devil. He may have done wrong, but I pity him. A jail within a jail. It is better he has gone. Maybe some day I, too, will journey to that happy land where there is no sorrow, pain, joy, or happiness.[11]

While Darl Shepherd was in jail, both he and Julie claimed that he was very ill from diabetes.[12] This was possibly a ploy for sympathy (inspired by Leo Koretz's plight?) in Shepherd's many fruitless attempts to get bail, as nothing before or after indicated that he had this disease.

Shepherd's normal personality was easygoing and laconic, but his feeling of confidence was perhaps aided by the fact that he had recently hired the "dream team" of defense attorneys: William Scott Stewart and William W. O'Brien, both in their mid-thirties. They had yet to lose a criminal case, and they tended to focus on high-profile trials. Their win-loss record by June 1925 was 28–0. Both would go on to become "mob lawyers," defending nearly all the top Chicago organized crime figures—including Al Capone.[13]

W. W. O'Brien had attained a degree of notoriety in 1921 when he was shot in a saloon and then refused to name the shooter—though it was evident that he knew who it was.[14] As this was standard behavior for mobsters ("we'll take care of this ourselves"), he was probably already connected with them.

In 1924, just a year before Shepherd's case, Stewart successfully defended Belva Gaertner when she was on trial for murdering her lover; and a month later, O'Brien won an acquittal for Beulah Sheriff Annan on the same charge.[15] Both women were accused of killing their paramours under the influence of gin and jazz, and the two trials—as well as the defendants themselves—were immensely popular in the media. Those who have seen the movie *Chicago*, winner of the 2002 Academy Award for Best Picture, know these two women as Velma Kelly (Gaertner) and Roxie Hart (Annan). The slick lawyer who defends them, Billy Flynn (played by Richard Gere), is an overdrawn caricature composite of Stewart and O'Brien, who were not above dirty tricks themselves.

Both attorneys were neat and well tailored in appearance, with O'Brien usually decked out in a colored shirt. William Scott Stewart looked younger than his years, and his perfectly appointed wardrobe led one reporter to dub him "the Beau Brummel of the courtroom." Stewart laughed a lot, while O'Brien was more nervous and serious. On cross-examination, Stewart employed a trick of putting his hands in his pockets in an "aw, shucks" manner, then—as reporter Genevieve Forbes Herrick described it—"swooping his head down [and] bringing it up slowly with a smile on his lips when he want[ed] to make a point." They both thrived on publicity and on media circuses and both had first-rate legal minds.[16]

Throughout the trial there was constant speculation about who was financing Shepherd's defense, as the estate funds were frozen until the trial was over and the will contest could be settled. There was a rumor, which Stewart and O'Brien did not deny, that the fee for the defense dream team would be half of the McClintock estate, which most people assumed would be at least $500,000.[17] And Robert Stoll had also put up quite a bit to finance his former partner's defense.[18]

But there was another source as well, and that was Carl Sigfrid. He had convinced a midwestern brokerage firm, Toombs & Daily, to loan Shepherd $50,000 in exchange for Shepherd's later investing the estate (which Toombs & Daily thought was $2,000,000) with the firm. Foolishly, they never had Shepherd sign a contract, but there was a gentlemen's agreement that the money would be paid back in the event of acquittal. It is possible that Sigfrid also arranged for other financing, or even provided some himself.[19]

Stewart and O'Brien's first move upon entering the Shepherd case was to claim that typhoid germs did not fall under the legal definition of poison, and that "no jury would send a dog to the pound on the testimony of Faiman."[20]

Back in Kenilworth, Julie Shepherd gave a three-hour interview to Genevieve Forbes Herrick of the *Chicago Tribune*, who at the young age of thirty-one already had a large reputation as a journalist. In 1921, in the spirit of Nellie Bly,[21] Herrick had gone underground to get a story on Ellis Island for the *Tribune*. The conditions she uncovered in her guise as an immigrant caused government officials to investigate and implement reform.[22]

Herrick also attended the court hearing in the matter of Leopold and Loeb throughout the summer of 1924. She had planned to marry fellow reporter John Origen Herrick on the weekend Judge Caverly intended to hand down his decision in the case, but she talked him into delaying it until after their wedding.[23]

Now Genevieve Forbes Herrick was assigned to cover the Shepherd case, with a focus on the defendant's wife, and she does not seem to have been overly impressed with the lady of the house.[24] In those articles, Julie is shown alternately as a drama queen and as coldly analytical, not as a sympathetic figure whose husband has been unjustly accused of the unthinkable crime of murdering the young man they were put in charge of.

Julie Shepherd told Herrick that what was being played out was a "dastardly scenario ... written by manifest liars in a frameup." There was a plot, she claimed, to "get the Shepherds"—or, more accurately, to get the Shepherds' money—and the plotters chose this way to do it rather than the more direct way of shooting them. As she spoke, an open Bible lay nearby, friends from the church were arranging flowers sent by well-wishers, and the Rev. Naumann (didn't he ever have parish duties to attend to?) presided over it all.

Even if what they said was true and Darl had really murdered Billy, Julie reasoned, would he have gone to a complete stranger like Faiman and exposed himself to blackmail? She does not seem to have considered the fact (or, if it occurred to her, to have expressed it) that Shepherd could hardly have gone to an acquaintance for help with his murder plot, if he really was guilty. Plus, he would need help getting the germs. Who better to approach than a con man whose credibility was already tainted by the nature of his "profession"?

Yet, for all her stand-by-your-man philosophy, Julie Shepherd never once visited her husband in jail. Observers were curious about this, and many felt it was because of her anger over the Sunshine Girl letters. The Shepherds insisted it was Darl's desire to spare his wife the distress of seeing him incarcerated.[25]

Nor was Julie herself immune from speculation as to her part in the murder scheme, if such there was. Many wondered aloud whether the death of her brother Otto in 1904, which resulted in Darl's complete ownership of the Salina drugstore, was a natural one. Perhaps the deadly duo had poisoned him. His death certificate shows that he died of complications from a long-standing rheumatic heart condition. No exhumation was ordered as a result of the accusations of poisoning.[26]

In fact, the irrepressible Judge Olson, never one to mince words, referred to Julie Shepherd as a "Lady Macbeth," the brains behind the McClintock scheme, "a cold, cruel pirate surrounded by a piratical crew; cold and purposeful," whereas Shepherd himself was "a soft and weak-willed man unable to make a living for himself and his wife."[27]

There is much to bolster this argument. Julie was smart and ambitious, shrewd at manipulating others to get what she wanted. Darl Shepherd was lazy and laid-back, perfectly content to let others feed and shelter him. As long as he didn't have to work too hard, or at all, he was satisfied with whatever life brought him. He does not seem to have been overly bright, whereas Julie was. Was it possible that she was the author of the plan and he was charged with carrying it out?

When she was told of Judge Olson's characterization of her as Lady Macbeth, Julie grew shrill: "That filthy beast! Judge Olson has a lust for human agony. When the end of this comes I shall not slink into a corner, but I shall be borne on the shoulders of the people."[28] (The *Sheboygan [Wisconsin] Press* felt the "filthy beast" appellation was inappropriate language for a lady.)[29]

In contrast to his wife's grandiose thinking was Darl Shepherd's reaction after his bail hearing, where his attorneys' request was denied. "Well, boys, I lost out," he told the jailers philosophically upon his return. "I guess I'll be with you a long time."[30] He was not in the least distressed by having to stay in jail, although possibly he was glad to have a break from Julie. If he had thoughts about the injustices being done to him, he did not voice them.

Later, Genevieve Forbes Herrick would aptly sum up both of these people, calling Julie Shepherd a "tall, commanding woman who reacts vividly to everything," while Darl was a "fattish acquiescent sort of man whose amiable enough indifference reacts to nothing."[31]

As the inquest ground on, each side accused the other of turning the courtroom into a "hippodrome" (today we could call this a media circus): Stewart and O'Brien wanted to put on witnesses who would testify to Marchand's being a drug addict, or "hophead," and to Faiman's being the same as well as an abortionist, while Crowe vehemently objected to this. ("You're trying to put on a hippodrome here.") For their part, the defense attorneys refused to allow their client to testify in what they called a "hippodrome atmosphere" because of witnesses whose credibility was suspect. Besides the allegations against Faiman and Marchand, Stewart and O'Brien also contended that Dr. Fosberg was an abortionist.[32]

But outside the courtroom is where the real circus was taking place. In Los Angeles, where she had gone to grieve in private, Isabelle Pope went from a weight of 125 pounds to 90.[33] But Judge Harry Olson, who referred to her (somewhat confusingly) as "one of the finest flowers of New England womanhood, of the Cal Coolidge type," worried that perhaps her weight loss was not due to a normal nervous illness[34]—possibly insinuating that she had been poisoned, a farfetched conclusion given the length of time she had been away from the Shepherds. Olson also said he had gotten another threatening phone call, and Earl Clark claimed to have been bribed by the defense to change his story.

Earl P. Clark said he was at National University one day when William D. Shepherd came in looking for Faiman, and he also heard Faiman phone Shepherd. Later, when the McClintock case was in the papers, Clark was present when John Marchand told about the letter having been sent by Shepherd to the school. Clark's testimony connected Shepherd to Faiman and also corroborated Marchand's story about the letter.

In late March 1925, Clark said he was approached by an operative of the Jones Detective Agency and offered $5,000 if he would retract his statement and then leave town with his wife until after the trial. In retaliation for this revelation, William Scott Stewart alleged that Judge Olson had done the bribing, offering Clark a job with the city if he left Chicago until the trial was over.[35] But Stewart's story makes no sense. Why would Olson *not* want Clark to testify to something that gave credence to Faiman's confession?

In fact, Dirty Deeds Done Dirt Cheap seems to have been the other name of the Jones Detective Agency. They constantly tried to tamper with the state's witnesses, with their intimidation and attempted kidnappings of Dr. Fosberg and Mrs. Olson; the propositions to Marchand, Clark, and others; and their threats when bribery would not work.

They even beat up one of their own operatives when they feared she had heard too much. Gladys Roberts was a twenty-two-year-old detective working for the Jones Agency, one of three women hired by them. She claimed that the agency also sold liquor as a sideline, which was illegal during Prohibition (it came to them from Washington DC through a railroad engineer). Shepherd had gone to the agency before his arrest to consult with John Jones, and Roberts listened through the keyhole. "You talk too much," she heard Jones tell Shepherd. "Get one story and stick to it and they'll never hook you." When he left the conference with Jones, Shepherd was "staggering drunk."

Gladys Roberts must have said something to someone about either the conference or the liquor. Jones told her she should have kept her mouth shut and not gotten mixed up in it. Shortly after that, Roberts was mugged by two men who showed no interest in her purse. For this reason, she thought it might have been done to convince her to keep quiet about the Shepherd case. Nonetheless, she continued to work for the Jones Agency.[36]

Mrs. Louise Olson, the doctor's widow (who seems to have been a particularly attractive target for the agency), said that one of the detectives posed as the emissary of a magazine and told her she had won a trip outside the country. The Jones Agency even admitted this, but never explained how it would have helped the defense to have Mrs. Olson unavailable. On yet another occasion they threatened that if she repeated anything her husband had told her, she would "never return alive" from the state's attorney's office.[37]

Another hippodrome-like incident was that of Mrs. Luella Rhuebell, who claimed to have been the business manager at National University, although other employees said they didn't know her. Rhuebell, calling Faiman "a monumental fakir [sic] and a dope fiend," said that no live germs were kept at the school, but only dead ones. (For a laboratory setting, however, it would have made no sense to have only dead germs on hand.)

Rhuebell herself was an interesting character. She and her room-mate, Ethel Stuart, once got drunk in their apartment and began brawling, which included hair-pulling and scratching. One gathers from the reports that this was not an unusual occurrence. Landlord W. C. Sedgwick couldn't break up the fight, so he had them arrested. While they were under the jurisdiction of the court, Sedgwick gathered together their effects because they still owed $57 in rent. These effects, Rhuebell claimed, included paperwork from National University (she never did produce it).

As a result of their fight, Rhuebell and Stuart were fined $5 each, plus costs, for disturbing the peace. Back in the apartment, Rhuebell then crawled out the window and down the fire escape when people from the state's attorney's office came to talk to her about Faiman and the school. She undoubtedly felt a great deal of loyalty to the defense, as William W. O'Brien paid her court fees, her $5 fine, and was giving her $20 a week for her eventual appearance at the Shepherd trial.[38]

But all of these sideshows would pale in comparison with the biggest event of all: the exhumation of the bodies of Judge Olson's brother, Dr. Oscar Olson, and Billy's mother, Emma McClintock, to determine whether they had been poisoned. The authorities were looking primarily for the metallic poisons, but they were unprepared for what they actually got: mercury in both bodies.[39]

Even the state's attorney's office was surprised at this, as neither victim exhibited the symptoms of mercury poisoning: tender gums, inflammation of the gastrointestinal system, vomiting, swollen salivary glands, and hemorrhaging.[40] It was eventually determined that Dr. Olson's body did not contain enough to have caused his death and was probably present in his medicine. But it was an entirely different case with Emma McClintock.

Mercury was used in several medicines of the day, especially as a cathartic, and was used externally as an antiseptic. Bichloride of mercury tablets, which were either blue or white, could be purchased in any drugstore without a prescription.[41] That mercury was an item normally found in the medicine chests of most homes can be seen in the unfortunate suicide of a teenager in Chicago in the spring of 1925, a student at Crane Technical High School who feared his ill health and poor academic performance had disappointed his parents. He took a large dose of bichloride of mercury.[42]

People often died of mercury poisoning when they ingested the tablets thinking they were something else. In 1913, in response to yet another accidental poisoning, a doctor wrote to the *New York Times* to say that there was no reason for anyone to have bichloride of mercury in the home. Doctors had a long list of much safer antiseptics, such as hydrogen peroxide, and if a patient needed to take a tablet internally as a tonic, it should be by prescription only. Another letter to the editor urged that the mercury tablets be sold in the blue pill only (the white pill looked like other, harmless medicine) and stamped "poison." But neither of these suggestions was acted on.[43]

At Christmastime 1924, a woman in Mississippi scraped bichloride of mercury from a tablet into some homemade fudge and sent it to her husband's son, who was living with his mother in New York. She was jealous of the attention her husband paid to her stepson and felt that he was neglecting her own son, who was living with them. However, the stepson was distracted by another gift in the Christmas box and did not eat the fudge. His aunt ate some and became immediately sick.[44]

Emma McClintock's autopsy in 1925 was performed sixteen years after her death, yet her body was remarkably intact.[45] Whereas at her funeral, witnesses said the skin had been black and swollen, now it was white. Only a slight darkening on the forehead indicated decomposition. Her clothing was intact, and the rouge on her cheeks—applied by the undertaker—was still visible.

Emma's organs were incredibly well preserved after such a long time. Even after sixteen years, enough mercury to kill two people was found in her stomach, liver, kidneys, and intestines. Its presence in her organs to this extent indicated that the poisoning had taken place approximately ten days before her death, probably in small doses. As she had not had convulsions, suicide and accidental overdose were ruled out.

Mrs. McClintock's physician, Dr. Krusemarck, said he had not given her any mercury, nor was this indicated by her heart problems. A check of her prescriptions confirmed this. The undertaker who embalmed her said that there was no mercury in the fluid.

The coroner concluded that Emma's heart problem was not the cause of her death and that, indeed, she would have lived many more years before succumbing to it. The cause of death was mercury poisoning of a homicidal nature.

Emma McClintock had died on June 7, 1909. That extended the ten-day window for the poison's effects to May 28, when she arrived in Bay View, Texas. The mercury would have been put in her food, or given to her as medicine, or put in medicine she was taking, which means it had to have been administered by someone she knew. There were witnesses in Texas who said that Darl Shepherd had given Emma pills and also liquid from a bottle while she was down there.[46]

As Shepherd was constantly dispensing medicine to those around him, nobody thought anything of it at the time or even after Emma died. Anna Anderson, one of Emma's maids, reported that although she had never seen Shepherd give medicine to Mrs. McClintock, Emma told her that he had.[47] Shepherd carried a medicine chest with him; and it was this item, among others, that Rev. Naumann collected from the Bay View home after Emma's death.[48] (There was also his incriminating question to Dr. Fosberg in 1924 about the detectability of bichloride of mercury after death. When he heard Fosberg's answer—that it stayed in the body for many years—he must have breathed a sigh of relief that there had been no autopsy when Emma died. He would not make that mistake with Billy.)

Shepherd's defense team tried to claim that Emma had been taking mercury that then accumulated in her body. But this was false for two reasons: she had not been taking any mercury-based medicines, and if she had, they would not have been present in her organs.

As for Judge Olson, he was not surprised that nothing was found in his brother's body. What he suspected was that prussic acid, a form of cyanide, had been administered to him, and that would have evaporated over the three years since the doctor's death.[49] He still maintained that, somehow, William Darling Shepherd had caused Oscar Olson's death.

However, while it is easy to see the motivation in Emma McClintock's murder, it is difficult to find one in Dr. Olson's. What would Shepherd have gained? Why would he do it when there were so many witnesses to his visit? Judge Olson was convinced that the motive was to keep his brother from telling Billy to make his own decisions and get away from the Shepherds as soon as he turned twenty-one. But Oscar had already done so, and several times, so the damage was already done. What possible benefit would there be to the Shepherds in his death?

Supposedly, Dr. Olson had told Harry's son Sanford that "Billy would never come into his fortune, but would die at Shepherd's hands."[50] Could this kind of talk have provided a motive to eliminate him?

Clearly, however, the circumstances of Emma McClintock's death point straight to Darl—and possibly Julie—Shepherd. They had the means, the motive, and the opportunity. Emma had gone to Bay View to confront Darl with his financial irresponsibility (at best) or thievery (at worst), and within days had come down with her final illness. She felt so bad that she left earlier than planned, arrived back in Chicago on June 3, and died four days later. To suppose that someone other than the Shepherds, with a motive never brought forward, had introduced bichloride of mercury into her food or medicine while she was in Bay View is to go against all reason.

After the autopsy of Emma McClintock, Coroner Oscar Wolff issued an arrest warrant for Julie Shepherd as an accessory to the murders of Emma and Billy McClintock. It was felt that she had at least guilty knowledge even if she was not an accomplice. But Julie got advance notice of the warrant and left the house with Robert Stoll before it could be served. She issued a statement that she had not wanted to spend the night in jail and would surrender herself to the sheriff.[51]

Surrender she did, with attorney (Stoll) in tow and miles of drama, too. Genevieve Forbes Herrick was scornful and sarcastic in her rendition of Julie's histrionics and her railing against "the most heathenish persecution I ever could dream of." Realizing that she was singled out by the coroner's jury precisely because she was Darl's wife, Julie also declared, "If Darl weren't my husband I never could stand this disgrace, this humiliation, the persecution of it all. But with him to think of the whole grim travesty becomes just another terrible blot of blackness packed down on me before the dawn that I know must come."[52]

Herrick thought her a "baffling feminine personality" in that her act could have been authentic or "strategic." The reporter's tone indicates that she thought it the latter: a lot of steely determination with just a soupçon of soft femininity thrown in to make herself more sympathetic. Julie's constant reference to Billy as "my boy," for example, could be a spontaneous reflection of her feelings for him or "an adroit bit of rhetoric." Her "deprecating gesture" while talking of Judge Olson was worthy of an actress. Regarding Julie's harping on Olson's "phobia" about the Shepherds ("He has Shepardphobia" and "He's trying to persecute us"), Herrick noted that "a cruel commentator" might say she had a similar obsession about Olson.[53]

Despite Julie's grand statements about her husband, she did nothing more than peck him briefly on the lips when she saw him for the first time in two months.[54] Perhaps the couple saved more intimate demonstrations for their short private meeting afterward.

It does beg credulity to think that this imperious, ironwilled woman could ever be strengthened in spirit by the lumpish dishrag that was her husband—a man who, by all appearances, did not seem to mind his plight too terribly.

When State's Attorney Robert Crowe heard about the arrest warrant issued for Julie Shepherd by Coroner Wolff, he was furious with Wolff and Judge Olson, both of whom he felt were trying to usurp his authority. He accused Wolff of thinking that the coroner's jury was the grand jury and accused Olson of thinking that he was the state's attorney. Crowe felt it would be difficult to get enough evidence against Julie to get an indictment, let alone a conviction. Therefore, he did not oppose the defense motion to release Julie on just a $5,000 bond, posted by her friend Mrs. Claudine Peterson.[55]

Claudine Peterson was the mother of Darl Shepherd's eighteen-year-old secretary, Eva, and most likely a relative of Carl Sigfrid, whose birth name had been Peterson. She was separated from her husband by 1925, but she was quite possibly Sigfrid's sister-in-law. Mrs. Peterson put up her house in Chicago for the bond.[56]

A few days later, the grand jury declined to indict Julie Shepherd because of a lack of evidence of her involvement in either death. She sobbed and denounced the "damnable, contemptible, satanical outrage" aimed at herself and her husband: "The hand of God saved me from this despicable plot and He will save my Darl." The reporter noted, as had Genevieve Forbes Herrick, that she always referred to Billy as "my boy," never by his name.[57]

Now completely free, Julie Shepherd vowed to take an active role in her husband's case. Stewart and O'Brien exuded a scornful confidence as they approached the trial date, May 18. Isabelle Pope wended her way back from California on the train to take her place on the witness stand. Chicago, still talking of Leopold and Loeb and of Belva and Beulah, readied itself for its fourth big trial in a year.

After several months of a stop-and-start inquest (consisting of seventy-five witnesses and 1,600 pages of testimony), of vituperative accusations, and of daily revelations of nefarious doings, the curtain was finally ready to go up in the case of *People of the State of Illinois v. William Darling Shepherd.*

Chapter 5

The State of Illinois v. William Darling Shepherd

In this town, murder's a form of entertainment.
—Mama Morton in the movie *Chicago*

Isabelle Pope, on her way to Chicago from California on the North Coast Limited with her Aunt Belle, was not eager to get on the witness stand. An immensely private person, she did not believe in airing personal matters in public, and she knew the attorneys on both sides would be fighting over her testimony. Nor was she looking forward to having all those memories of Billy stirred up.

Isabelle was a firm believer in letting God settle accounts, so she refrained from overtly criticizing the Shepherds when talking to reporters. Still, some of her negative feelings seeped out. She couldn't understand why the Shepherds had left so soon after Billy's death, she told *Chicago Tribune* reporter Maureen McKernan. As for Julie Shepherd's Bible quoting—well, that only appeared over the preceding year when Julie seemed to acquire a "marked religious disposition" around the time of Billy's twenty-first birthday. Isabelle had plenty of opportunities to see the Shepherds over the four years she dated Billy, and there were never any Bible references before that time.

As Isabelle talked to Maureen McKernan about Billy, she inadvertently slipped into the present tense, describing his many attributes and wistfully talking of their plans. She showed the reporter a picture of Billy in knickers and what she called his "funny, hectic socks."[1]

But, as Isabelle Pope was preparing for (and dreading) her role as witness, another important witness came up missing. Robert White, an employee (actually Faiman's bodyguard) at National University, had given a statement to State's Attorney Crowe about having seen Faiman and Shepherd together at the school. This testimony was important because it validated what both Faiman and Marchand were saying. Now, however, just as jury selection was about to begin, White, his wife, and his two children were gone.[2]

An investigation revealed that White had gone to see defense attorney William O'Brien in his office, then rented a car from the newly established Hertz Drive-Ur-Self System, gathered up his family, and left for parts unknown. William Scott Stewart claimed to have an affidavit from White wherein he recanted his statement about seeing Shepherd at the school and asserted that Crowe had threatened White that he would never see his family again if he didn't say what they wanted him to say. But the defense refused to produce this affidavit, then later admitted it was just a signed statement and not really an affidavit. The document held by Stewart consisted of four wrinkled sheets, but he would not let anyone look at them.

Robert White's landlady had a different story. She said that when White had come back from identifying Shepherd, he told her he had recognized him immediately: "I can never forget those bulging eyes," he said at the time. A friend of White's wife received a letter that said the family had to flee because agents of the defense had threatened them.

After this, various people—mostly connected with the newspapers—were sent letters purporting to be from the missing witness White and postmarked from Philadelphia. As White had relatives in New York City, it was felt that he was using Philadelphia post offices to keep from being found. He had not been bribed as had been reported, White wrote, but he had been threatened and this was why he left. The defense forced him to sign the document contradicting his original statement and, to make sure it stayed that way, they sent three tough guys to "persuade" him: Art Byrne, James J. Kelley or Kelly (also known as Riley or O'Reilly), and "Jew" Golden. (Crowe said Golden was a beer runner and "all around bad man.")

Chicago investigators found White's rental car in Greenwich Village with some family belongings in the trunk, including a crying doll. They found it because White, who was concerned about not having returned the car when he was supposed to, sent the paperwork to Judge Thomas J. Lynch, who would be presiding over the trial, and included a note to the Hertz Company telling them where the car was and why he could not return it himself.

White's letters, which were the source of much amusement in the press, were an odd mixture of beautiful handwriting and grammatical errors, and it was thought that he had dictated them to his wife or someone else. For some, he used the title "Dr." before his name (probably a title he used at National University). Writing to Assistant State's Attorney Joseph Savage, he insisted that his original statement about seeing Shepherd was the truth:

> Mr. Savage, don't think for one moment that I am telling you all this looking for sympathy because that's not the case. The true facts are and always will be is either go or get killed and write a statement what we tell you to and Kelly told them what other things to put in that statement.[*sic*]

In his letter to John Hertz, enclosed in his letter to Judge Lynch (why didn't he just send the paperwork and directions to Hertz?), White was unintentionally humorous:

> Drive-it-yourself and that's what you will have to do because Robert E. Crowe, State's Attorney, will not let me drive it back to Chicago; he wants the honor of bringing me back with it and a detective.

But it turned out that White *was* in Pennsylvania after all, at least for part of the time: he had been arrested for forging a grocer's name to some checks and was cooling his heels in a Pittsburgh jail.[3] He eventually did return to Chicago in time for the testimony phase of the trial.

White's adventure was not the only accusation of dirty tricks leveled at Shepherd's defense team. While prospective jurors were being questioned, Crowe began receiving reports of attempted bribery. In the most blatant attempt, excused venireman Philip Barry said that he had been approached by a longtime Chicago precinct captain, James C. "Cal" Callan, who told him he was working for Stewart and O'Brien. Barry had known him for about eighteen years. Callan directed Barry to make sure he got on the jury: "You would make a good juror for Shepherd and we will make it worth your while. Who's your best friend? I'm no fool and I'm not talking to a fool."

However, Barry, who was a former head of the Department of Justice in Chicago (so you have to wonder what Callan was thinking in approaching him), told the trial attorneys that he had a fixed opinion in the Shepherd matter and was let go, as were all those with opinions.

This was not Callan's first attempt at jury tampering. He had once been brought before the grand jury to testify against a man accused of murder, an officer in the Sheet Metal Workers Union. Callan refused to testify and later went around to various state's witnesses, threatening them to "keep your damned mouth shut."[4]

Callan was arrested for his attempt in the Shepherd case and brought up on charges of contempt of court. At the hearing, Crowe and the defense attorneys fired off salvos at each other. Crowe accused them of "trying to get a lot of crooks on Shepherd's jury," and in return Stewart demanded that he be allowed to cross-examine Barry to "show that he does not tell the truth."

Stewart disrupted the proceedings so often with this that the judge threatened him with contempt. He had no legal standing at this hearing, which Crowe pointed out to him, "unless you want to claim fathership of Callan." Crowe was fairly shouting at this point, and Stewart shouted right back: "I certainly would not claim fathership of Faiman!" Stewart went on to say that he wouldn't even want Barry on his jury because he didn't think he would be fair. "I don't think he's honest," he concluded, and Crowe shot back, "No, you don't want any honest men on the jury." Stewart had obviously run out of snappy ripostes, as all he could come up with was, "Oh, you'd like to have honest men on the jury, I suppose."[5]

After this incident, Crowe vowed to investigate all jurors, and even their wives, who were involved in any case of Stewart and O'Brien going back over the previous six months. One of the veniremen for the Shepherd trial admitted to taking a bribe in a labor conspiracy case where he had sat as a juror, but this does not seem to have been a Stewart and O'Brien trial. But Crowe's investigators did turn up a perjuring witness who had helped in the acquittal of a Stewart-O'Brien client.[6]

So jury selection, all things considered, was not going well. Apart from the attempts at jury fixing, there seemed to be a feeling among the lawyers that anyone who had read any of the accounts of the case in the newspapers was not a fit juror.

This meant they were pretty much looking for people who didn't read newspapers, as the Shepherd case was on the front pages nearly every day, and for most of that time was the main headline.

A *New York Times* editorial from May 30, when 190 men had been examined and only 3 selected for the jury to date, decried this approach:

> And what is it that defense and prosecution are trying to get? Why, jurymen of such demonstrated unintelligence and so little interest in what is going on around them that they have not formed ... an opinion in a case that has received a large amount of attention from everybody with enough sense to be justified in deciding a question of life and death.[7]

Even though the lawyers seemed to be looking for the clueless and the ignorant, one prospective juror was dismissed for "insufficient schooling."[8] Another was excused because he had been on the "Black Sox" jury, when eight members of the Chicago White Sox were acquitted of conspiring to throw the 1919 World Series, despite the fact that they had confessed to doing so.[9] A courtroom spectator, obviously a connoisseur of high-profile murder trials, walked out during the jury selection because it was "a damned dull show." Through it all, William D. Shepherd snoozed peacefully.[10]

When the fourth juror was selected, the man's wife sent word to the court that if he were kept on the jury she would kill herself by turning on the gas in her home. Judge Lynch sent a doctor to their house to check it out. The doctor returned with a verdict of "self-induced hysteria" and the husband was kept on the jury. It was not reported what the wife did about this.[11]

William Scott Stewart took advantage of the voir dire process to tell the jury pool that Judge Olson had concocted the whole case against Shepherd so he could get some of the McClintock estate money for himself and for his brother Oscar's widow. Stewart maintained that Olson had cut a deal with the McClintock heirs, who were contesting the will: "Judge Olson is not on the square," he told the panel. "He is vicious and vindictive."[12]

In the press, Stewart and O'Brien issued a colorful statement as jury selection was grinding slowly forward:

> The conspiracy against Shepherd is a house of cards and is being blown to pieces and to the four corners of the earth by the four winds of truth. The case is obviously a frame-up, simple but not pure.[13]

Julie Shepherd had determined that she would sit in back of her husband every day to show her support and made the mistake of announcing this in the newspaper. Crowe was equally determined that she would *not* do this, and when she showed up in court on the first day of jury selection and was told to sit elsewhere, she threw a veritable tantrum. William Scott Stewart had to calm her down. Crowe's rationale was that she would influence the jury unduly, but a more subtle agenda was undoubtedly to deprive Darl Shepherd of his support system.[14]

Finally, after three weeks and three days, with 900 men examined, the jury was set on June 10. It consisted of a street car motorman, a laundry driver, a renting agent, a roundhouse foreman, an automobile mechanic, a proofreader, a purchasing agent, a florist, a hoisting engineer, a salesman, a railroad treasurer, and a bank-vault keeper—all men, as had always been the case and was still the tradition, even though women had by then been enfranchised.[15]

While selection had been going on, Roald Amundsen's plane was reported missing. Amundsen, who was trying to be the first to fly over the North Pole—and would succeed—turned up safe and on course a few days later (although he would not be so lucky just three years later, when his plane disappeared on another flight).[16]

Angelo Genna, the first of the three brothers who would eventually be killed by Bugs Moran, was gunned down in May, just four months after his wedding day, as part of Moran's retaliation for the November murder of Dion O'Banion. Genna, whose wedding cake in January weighed 2,000 pounds, now had a solid silver coffin worth $11,000 with his name in gold letters. There was $50,000 worth of flowers. Al Capone, who had ordered the hit on O'Banion and so was somewhat responsible for the murders of the Genna brothers, sent lilies.[17] Angelo Genna was buried approximately twenty yards from his old enemy, Dion O'Banion, causing one funeral-goer to speculate on what a raucous event Judgment Day might be in Mt. Carmel Cemetery when the two mobsters exited their tombs and saw each other.[18]

That June, Richard Loeb was put in the Joliet Prison hospital, delirious from measles. It was thought that the extent of his disease and delirium made him hopelessly insane, but he eventually recovered.[19] In North Carolina, fifty-four miners died in the Coal Glen Mine Disaster.[20] A young Dayton, Tennessee, high school teacher, John T. Scopes, was indicted for teaching evolution to his science classes. (Clarence Darrow would represent him, and the silver-tongued orator William Jennings Bryan would prosecute. Bryan died during the trial that summer.)[21] An amateur wrestler in Connecticut, diagnosed with cancer, chose a unique way to end his life. He got into a baby carriage at the top of a hill and, as it rolled down, shot himself in the head. After it crashed into a pole at the bottom, his distraught wife wheeled his body, still in the baby carriage, to a neighbor's house.[22]

A proposed bill in the Illinois legislature sought to forbid murderers to inherit from their victims, a practice that exists in all states today but did not at the time of the Shepherd case.[23] Backers of the new bill cited the case of Ray Pfanschmidt, a twenty-year-old Quincy, Illinois, boy who was accused of murdering his parents, his fifteen-year-old sister, and a twenty-one-year-old visitor. Pfanschmidt's father was a wealthy farmer who was also heavily insured, and Ray inherited the estate after eventually being acquitted of the crimes. Despite the acquittal, most people felt he had murdered his family for the money.[24]

Finally, the witness phase of *Illinois v. Shepherd* was ready to begin. Hundreds of people lined up outside the courthouse, ready for the next big Chicago sensation. After the Leopold-Loeb trial, a rule had gone into effect banning photographs in the courtroom, but many reporters smuggled in cameras under their coats and took surreptitious pictures. Playing "hide and seek" with the bailiffs, who were determined to enforce the new rule, photographers used very small vest pocket cameras. When they wanted to take a picture, they took it quickly and returned the camera to its hiding place as the bailiffs sought in vain to determine the source. Every day, newspapers carried scores of these photos that had been taken in the courtroom in spite of the rule.[25]

Because there would be much nationwide interest in the Millionaire Orphan case, "Dad" Watson, the court caretaker, strung up Western Union wires in a separate room, where he also provided extra telephones and typewriters. For Chicago and national reporters, seventy-five camp chairs were set up in the front of the courtroom.[26]

The prosecution team would be the same as for the Leopold-Loeb case: State's Attorney Robert E. Crowe and Assistant State's Attorneys Joseph P. Savage and George E. Gorman, along with John Sbarbaro, the nephew of the former restaurant owner who had had the oyster conversation with Shepherd. Sbarbaro would focus on the bacteriology issue because he had some medical school and undertaking experience in his background.

The defense team would be William Scott Stewart and the former actor William W. O'Brien, who had hinted that their client might not even take the stand. The truth was that Shepherd did not want to, probably because of his fear of being tripped up in cross-examination. But his attorneys must have seen that he had no charm, no sympathetic personality to attract a jury, and possibly concurred in this decision. He was just a slow-moving, overweight buffoon, and maybe would do himself more harm than good up against a skilled cross-examiner like Robert Crowe. But on the plus side for the defense, would a jury believe that a zero like Shepherd could concoct this plot and carry out such an extraordinary scheme? So they would reserve their decision on his testifying for later in the trial.

The presiding judge was forty-six-year-old Thomas J. Lynch, elected to the circuit court in 1921. Before that he had been an alderman and had served on the city council. Lynch presided over a lot of divorce cases and in 1923 was the judge in Louis Armstrong's. (One of Lynch's favorite sayings was, "Alimony is as out of date as the horse and buggy.")[27]

The charges against Shepherd included not only murder by typhoid, but also murder by aconite, morphine, and prussic acid, alone and in combination with typhoid infection. It was thought that Billy's death almost immediately after Isabelle's procuring the marriage license might indicate that Shepherd had hastened the death by one of these drugs so the wedding could not take place.[28] According to Dr. Fosberg's testimony, Shepherd had shown an interest in the undetectability of prussic acid after death.

Aconite, or aconitine, known in the plant world as monkshood, became a popular staple of murder mysteries: since it is a plant, it can be placed in a harmless-looking salad, or its roots can be served as radishes. Aconite depresses the central nervous system and eventually shuts down the heart. In the Middle Ages, it was smeared on arrows to poison the enemy in the event he survived the wound.[29]

Morphine is also a depressant and would have either killed Billy if given in sufficient dosage or caused unconsciousness so he could be smothered with a pillow.

Prussic acid is a form of cyanide and prevents the body's red blood cells from taking in oxygen—in effect, it suffocates them. This was the poison purchased by Massachusetts murderer Lizzie

Borden to kill off her stepmother and her father. When this didn't work (they didn't use the sugar she put it in), she axed them to death. Cyanide gas was used by the Nazis in their concentration camps and is today used in execution gas chambers.[30] However, the victim of cyanide poisoning typically manifests a skin color that ranges from pink to cherry red,[31] and nobody ever mentioned that Billy's corpse was this color. It is noticeable, as it makes the deceased look alive and healthy, so someone probably would have commented on it even if he or she were unaware of the cyanide connection.

All three of these substances—aconite, morphine, and prussic acid—would have evaporated fairly quickly from the body after death and so be undetected. However, if prussic acid had been used and if Billy had been autopsied right away, which he was not, it might have been possible for someone to detect the bitter almond smell that is the hallmark of cyanide poisoning. Not everyone is able to smell this, so even that might have gone undetected.[32]

In late May, Judge Harry Olson received a book on poisons from Houston's chief of police, who in turn had received it from a Mrs. Nichols. She said it had belonged to William Darling Shepherd and that the notations were in his handwriting, but as the book was never offered into evidence, it was probably a spurious claim.[33]

Robert Crowe's opening statement for the prosecution detailed the activities of the Shepherds vis-à-vis the McClintocks from the death of William Sr. to the death of William Jr. and endeavored to present these as part of a plan, scheme, and design to wrest the Fatal Fortune from the McClintocks. His second sentence was, "This is a murder case," and as he spoke the words there was an ominous clapping of thunder and flashing of lightning outside the courtroom windows.[34]

Crowe called the Shepherds parasites and murderers and greedy schemers (he did not exclude Julie even though she was not on trial), but when he called them panhandlers, they were irate. It was this term they resented the most, although even their own attorneys characterized them as lazy.[35]

Jury selection had taken just over three weeks. The entire rest of the trial would take only two, and the biggest puzzle of it all was the prosecution's case: whom they chose to exclude and whom they chose to have testify. For example, the first witness was Judge Olson, whose bulldog investigation had kept the coroner's inquest alive for many months and had led to the current trial. Yet, the only questions Crowe had for him on direct examination concerned his relationship with the three McClintocks (although Olson had known Emma, he had only seen William and Billy a couple of times) and the fact that he had no direct knowledge of the cause of Billy's death.

Olson's brief time on the stand was not without fireworks, as the defense attorneys were like tigers waiting to pounce on the man they saw as the instigator of the plot against the Shepherds. With Crowe's first question ("Did you know Emma Nelson McClintock in her lifetime?"), there was an objection by Stewart. Olson, later claiming he didn't hear the objection, answered it without waiting for the judge's ruling, which then sent both Stewart and O'Brien into a frenzy. They scolded him for answering, which then angered Judge Olson: "I object to the remarks of counsel." O'Brien retorted, "All right. I object to him objecting," and Olson countered with "I don't have to be insulted because I am a judge." Judge Lynch had to take over and soothe everyone's egos.[36]

There was a humorous exchange between Judge Olson and W. W. O'Brien concerning Olson's contact with Billy's father. Although Olson had seen McClintock Sr. several times around town, he had only spoken to him once, "at the funeral." O'Brien, thinking he meant at McClintock's own funeral, asked incredulously, "You did not talk to him at his funeral, did you?" It turned out that Olson meant Emma's mother's funeral.[37]

Although Judge Olson had no direct knowledge of Billy's death, he did have direct knowledge of many things unearthed in the investigation that followed—an investigation that he had instigated. Yet, none of this was brought out by the prosecution, and consequently could not be addressed by the defense. After the trial, Crowe said his purpose in putting the judge on was so the defense could cross-examine him and not later complain that they didn't have access to the source of the alleged plot against their client. However, cross-examination is limited to matters brought up during direct examination, and Crowe had not opened many doors in this regard.

Another puzzling witness was Estelle Gehling, the Sunshine Girl. Although she said there were letters she had received from Shepherd voicing his concern about being "out in the street" when Billy got married, she was not asked to produce these. The only letter put in evidence was the one from October 1924 where he talked about a big deal falling through and bankrupting him. The defense did not even bother to cross-examine Gehling, as this would have called attention to the love affair. She had done so little damage during her four minutes on the stand that it was undoubtedly a wise move on their part.[38]

Alexander F. Reichmann detailed the problems incurred with the Shepherds over the raising of Billy. William Scott Stewart's cross-examination focused on Reichmann's friendship with Judge Olson; John Lee, Isabelle Pope's attorney; and Orville Taylor, attorney for the McClintock heirs. The insinuation was that these lawyers constituted the Evil Empire that was conspiring to keep the McClintock fortune away from the Shepherds by concocting the "poisoning by typhoid" accusation. Reichmann grew indignant at Stewart's suggestion that he had grown wealthy from the McClintock trust and asked Judge Lynch to protect him against such accusations. Robert Crowe angrily called Stewart a "shyster."[39]

There were a few witnesses who told of Shepherd's attempts to undermine Reichmann by saying that the trust attorney told him he wanted to get "a slice of the McClintock fortune" (as if the reputable and very proper Reichmann would ever make such a statement—true or not—to someone like Shepherd). There was also Jerome Matillo's testimony that "Willie will come out with his pockets full," and then the medical witnesses who treated Billy while alive and autopsied him after death.

Louis Sbarbaro repeated his 1917 conversation with Shepherd about where the poison was located in an oyster. A cashier from Shepherd's bank brought in the defendant's records to show how very little in savings he ever had (most of the time $1 or less).[40] Some of the servants testified as to the Shepherds' behavior and the presence of Darl's own personal laboratory, complete with tubes and Bunsen burner. Two reporters told of their interviews with Shepherd right after Billy's death, where he gave two different versions of what Billy's will contained—neither of them correct.

A colorful witness named Beulah Allred of Oklahoma (dubbed "The Cowgirl" by the press) testified that Shepherd was acquainted with a typhoid specialist, Dr. Margaret Bodek. Allred herself knew Shepherd because she had been involved in a land deal with him. After her testimony, The Cowgirl decided to stay on in Chicago and do detective work for the prosecution.[41]

There was proof of the connection between Dr. Bodek and the Shepherds, although it was not presented at the trial: in March

1921, Dr. Bodek transferred a half interest in 100 acres of Arkansas land for $1 to Julie Shepherd and Thomas A. Newman, the editor friend who had accompanied them on their visit to Dr. Oscar Olson the night he died.[42] Dr. Bodek herself was never called to testify, but it would have been one more link connecting the Shepherds with a knowledgeable source concerning typhoid.

Much of this testimony consisted of small pieces of circumstantial evidence that, taken individually, amounted to nothing, but when put together formed a diabolical picture. The "big guns," on the other hand, would present more direct evidence of murder: Dr. Frank Breidigan, Dr. Amante Rongetti (a new witness who had just come forward), Isabelle Pope, John P. Marchand, and—the grand finale—Charles C. Faiman. Notably absent from this list was Dr. George Fosberg.

Dr. Breidigan, the Kellogg's Sanitarium bacteriologist, once again told of his encounters with Shepherd while head of the Illinois Research Laboratory. The cross-examination brought out nothing except that many visitors to the lab were curious about it (although they undoubtedly did not return again and again to ask more questions).[43]

Dr. Amante Rongetti was an interesting character who was acquainted with Charles Faiman. He and Faiman had had some personal difficulties, primarily over Rongetti's wife, although the testimony he would give for the prosecution substantiated Faiman's. Rongetti said that Shepherd had approached him in 1923 and wanted to take a course in bacteriology. Shepherd supposedly wanted to know how typhoid could get into the body.

The defense tried to introduce evidence of Rongetti's prior conviction for an unspecified crime, but was not allowed to get it in. However, the crime was most likely the performing of an abortion, with the patient possibly dying as a result of it, as Rongetti had legal difficulties with this after the trial.

But Rongetti had made the whole thing up. He originally thought of going to the defense to see if he could get some money by testifying for them (word of this may have tipped the defense to his current perjury), but ended up with the state instead. On cross-examination, he demonstrated almost no knowledge of bacteriology. When it began to look as if he had not talked to Shepherd at all, he tried to hedge by saying that, although the man he spoke with was quite a bit thinner than the defendant, he thought he was the same one. Finally, he admitted that nobody at all had approached him about typhoid or bacteriology.[44]

The day that Isabelle Pope was to testify, the courtroom was crowded with hundreds of pushing and shoving spectators—mostly women—curious to see the grieving fiancee. The fact that she was both young and beautiful made her a tragic figure in the McClintock-Shepherd drama.

Isabelle was tastefully dressed in a modest black outfit with just a touch of white and blue in relief. She wore a cloche-type hat, a stone marten fur around her neck, and the diamond engagement ring given her by Billy. She never smiled throughout her testimony and was neither dramatic nor overly emotional. She spoke so quietly that she could barely be heard beyond the witness stand.[45]

While Isabelle was on the stand, Darl Shepherd never looked at her. Usually bland and impassive during testimony, he showed agitation for the first time, nervously drinking water and shuffling papers.[46]

Under cross-examination Isabelle was patient and never lost her temper. But the defense nonetheless managed to take some of the luster from her shining reputation by painting her as a mercenary gold-digger whose motive in wanting a deathbed marriage was to get Billy's fortune. This, of course, was not true, but when under questioning by Stewart she admitted cutting a 50/50 deal with the heirs who were contesting the will, and there was an audible gasp in the courtroom. Gone was her image as a perfectly innocent, naive young woman thwarted in her romance by the wicked stepparents.

Isabelle also made the mistake many of us do, unwittingly, when we realize that things are not as we had thought they were: we revise the past and put a construction on it that was not necessarily there at the time, because we don't like to think we have been fooled by people or by circumstances. ("Oh, I knew all the time she was up to no good.") On direct examination, Isabelle indicated that the Shepherds were cold to her once they knew she and Billy would be getting married, and she said she did not feel welcome in their home. But Stewart made her read portions of her own letters to Billy, where she expressed to him how well she was getting along with them and doing things with Mrs. Shepherd while Billy was away at Dartmouth.[47]

What Isabelle was doing, of course, was a perfectly natural thing in letting her present knowledge of what the Shepherds were up to color her past recollection of them. She may also have been concerned that painting them in too rosy a light would hurt the state's chances of getting a conviction. The result, however, was to diminish her credibility as a witness.

Actually, the defense had guessed right in thinking that Isabelle was being influenced by those around her to get involved in the will contest. At first she was going to sue for a widow's share, since, but for the Shepherds' interference, she would have married Billy on his deathbed. Later, in exchange for her not pursuing this, she made the deal with the heirs to join with them. This plan—the widow's suit—had been thought up by Judge Olson and Isabelle's two attorneys, John H. S. Lee and John J. Healy, as a way to prevent the Shepherds from enjoying their ill-gotten gains.

All along the way, these men told Isabelle that she needed to "do this for Billy," to bring him justice.[48] She went along with it because of that, but would have been happier to stay out of the limelight. Still, she never lost her cool on the stand or in the newspapers, never engaged in verbal battles with anyone, and remained dignified throughout the whole ordeal. But the cross-examination and what it revealed caused the media and the public to become disenchanted with her.

Regarding Isabelle's testimony as to what Shepherd had told her of his studies of typhoid and the statistics from the Spanish-American War, Stewart asked her if she were not aware that Shepherd's brother had been a physician in that war—hence his quite natural interest in the subject.[49] Isabelle could not recall any such statement from him. The state let this go unchallenged, but, indeed, the question should have been asked: which brother would that have been? Preston the painter/paperhanger? Henry the bicycle repairman? Neither of these men was a doctor, nor had either one been in the Spanish-American War.[50] Yet the jury was left with a reasonable explanation of Shepherd's interest in typhoid that was completely false—and completely uncontested.

Patrick J. McMahon/John P. Marchand then told his story of talking to Shepherd about the latter's letter of inquiry to the National University of Sciences. On direct examination, Marchand revealed a potpourri of occupations he had engaged in, even though he was only in his early thirties: machinist, cooper, distillery worker, bell hop, railroad worker, soldier, barber, salesman.[51]

Marchand came across as a wise guy, a man with a chip on his shoulder, which undoubtedly influenced his credibility with the jury. The defense revealed that he was being put up at the

Briggs House, and the state's attorney's office was paying for this. He was also being paid $50 a week by them because he was unable to work while waiting to testify. He had an attitude of defiance when he admitted this, as if it were something he was entitled to.

Marchand tended to respond to questions with questions of his own, and when O'Brien tried to destroy his credibility with insinuations of extortion and drug use, the following exchange occurred:

O'Brien: Was it your plan to sell [the letter of inquiry] for [$100,000]?
Marchand: If it had been, I wouldn't have talked about it.
O'Brien: You didn't expect any money from it?
Marchand: Would I have been talking about it?
O'Brien: Do you use dope?
Marchand: Do I look like it?
O'Brien: Yes, sir.
Marchand: Good.

Of course, the star witness of the trial was, and always had been, Charles C. Faiman. The prosecution saved him until last and then, in an incredibly self-destructive move, asked the court to call him as its own witness because the state did not wish to vouch for him.[52] Today, attorneys are protected from witnesses who change their testimony on the stand: they are allowed to ask the court to declare that the witness is "hostile," and they can then cross-examine to show the discrepancies between the two testimonies.

There was no such protection in Illinois in 1925. Crowe was afraid that Faiman would recant his statements about Shepherd and that would be the end of the trial. He wanted to be able to cross-examine him if this occurred so the jury could see that he was most likely perjuring himself. This would allow the trial to go on, as the jury could then choose to believe Faiman's original incriminating statements against Shepherd. In other words, the prosecution did not want to "own" Faiman and be bound by what he said.

This was the biggest mistake made by the state in the trial. Since the request was made in front of the jury, the message, loud and clear, was, "We don't quite believe this next witness so we don't want to be bound by his testimony." The legal subtleties of what Crowe was trying to do were beyond the comprehension of laymen. He would have been better off putting Faiman on and hoping for the best. Because, as it turned out, Faiman made a pretty good witness.

Faiman's strengths as a witness were an incredible knowledge of bacteriology, so that there were no flaws in what he said he told Shepherd; a calm and patient demeanor that did not get rattled even in the face of caustic cross-examination; and a refusal to be shaken in any aspect of his testimony. Even the *Chicago Tribune* grudgingly acknowledged that "he might be a charlatan but not a perjurer."[53]

As with the appearance of Isabelle Pope on the witness stand, the courtroom was packed to hear the testimony of Faiman ("the squealer"). He was, of course, impeccably dressed. In fact, he came back after the lunch break wearing an entirely different set of clothes—just as stylish as those he had worn for the morning session.[54] It was as if he wanted to let people know that, whatever else he might be, he was definitely a financial success.

On the stand, Charles Faiman spoke so softly that the overhead fan had to be turned off so he could be heard. Jurors and spectators leaned forward, cupping their ears, and still it was difficult. One reporter complained that he seemed to be "talking into his lap" for most of his testimony.[55]

Faiman admitted he had initially lied to the state's attorney about knowing Shepherd. He admitted giving out diplomas to those who merely paid a fee and never attended classes. But he stood firm in his statement that he gave vials of typhoid to William Darling Shepherd and showed him how to keep them alive: he told him the germs would have to be fed with agar once a month, but that this was easily procured at any drugstore. In lieu of agar, egg whites would suffice.

Faiman insisted that he could walk into the Department of Health and procure germs from the clerks there, and had done so several times. He claimed not to know their names, but he was probably protecting them, as anybody he named would surely have been without a job the next day.

The defense tried its best to impeach Faiman with his misdeeds regarding the selling of drugs and alcohol, but Judge Lynch refused to let this in. They did get him to admit that he was a "corn doctor" (quack), with no license to practice medicine. The cross-examination reveals something else as well, albeit between the lines: the true role probably taken by Faiman in the plot to murder Billy McClintock.

As Shepherd asked him more and more questions about typhoid, Faiman said he began chatting with him about his personal life. Did he have a family? Shepherd told him about his foster son, the millionaire. "That must be pretty nice for you, having a wealthy boy like that," Faiman commented, then speculated on what would happen to Shepherd if the boy got married, how Darl and Julie would be out in the cold.

"What's that to you?" was Stewart's question to Faiman on cross-examination. "What did you care whether the boy got married or not?" Faiman had few answers to these questions, other than "just making conversation," and for some he remained silent. But Faiman's conversations with Shepherd reveal that the con man was fishing for what the typhoid germs would be used for. He had sensed that this was not an innocent inquiry on Shepherd's part and was letting him know that he was not fooled by it. He was also inviting Shepherd to confide in him. Herein lies the real reason Faiman didn't ask to be paid for giving the lessons: he had plans for a bigger cut once the typhoid germs did their awful deed.

Then the state rested. Crowe had not brought in Dr. Fosberg to reinforce Faiman's and Breidigan's statements. He had not brought in Robert White, who had absconded with the Hertz rental car, to connect Faiman and Shepherd. He had not brought in Louis Kles, the former Shepherd chauffeur who had seen Darl's special laboratory at least twice. Nor did he introduce Faiman's letter to the architect outlining the plans for a $100,000 university building.

The defense team had been handed an unexpected gift. Could they use it to help their client?

Billy McClintock as a child with his mother, Emma Nelson McClintock. (*Chicago Daily News* negatives collection, DN-078794. Courtesy of the Chicago Historical Society.)

Isabelle Pope as a teenager. (Courtesy of the family of Isabelle Pope.)

The Phi Delta Theta fraternity at Dartmouth College. Billy is fourth from the left in the first row. (Courtesy of the family of Isabelle Pope.)

Picture of "my Billy boy" taken by
Isabelle Pope: "He was just right.
Just tall enough to look fine—just
taller than me—just heavy enough,
and his hair was just crinkled
enough. He's so sweet." (Courtesy
of the family of Isabelle Pope.)

Isabelle Pope. (Courtesy of the family of Isabelle Pope.)

Julie Shepherd flanked by Rev. Carl A. Naumann (left) and attorney Robert H. Stoll. (*Chicago Daily News* negatives collection, DN-078751. Courtesy of the Chicago Historical Society.)

The prosecution team from the State's Attorney's office (seated, left to right: George Gorman, Robert Crowe, Joseph Savage; standing in back: John Sbarbaro). (*Chicago Daily News* negatives collection, DN-078768. Courtesy of the Chicago Historical Society.)

Julie and Darl Shepherd. (*Chicago Daily News* negatives collection, DN-078310. Courtesy of the Chicago Historical Society.)

Judge Harry Olson makes a point to the jury. (*Chicago Daily News* negatives collection, DN-078771. Courtesy of the Chicago Historical Society.)

Dr. George Fosberg on the stand at the inquest. (*Chicago Daily News* negatives collection, DN-079281. Courtesy of the Chicago Historical Society.)

Rev. Carl Naumann, pastor of St. Mark's Lutheran Church in Evanston. (*Chicago Daily News* negatives collection, DN-079186. Courtesy of the Chicago Historical Society.)

Charles C. Faiman. (*Chicago Daily News* negatives collection, DN-078722. Courtesy of the Chicago Historical Society.)

Estelle Gehling, the "Sunshine Girl." (*Chicago Daily News* negatives collection, DN-078781. Courtesy of the Chicago Historical Society.)

Carl J. Sigfrid in a photo taken around 1910. (Courtesy of Ouray County, Colorado, Historical Society.)

Billy McClintock in a picture taken by
Isabelle Pope. (Courtesy of the family
of Isabelle Pope.)

Shepherd and his defense attorneys, William Scott Stewart (left) and
William W. O'Brien. (*Chicago Daily News* negatives collection, DN-
078745. Courtesy of the Chicago Historical Society.)

Julie in the courtroom with Elsie Gunn, Rev. Carl Naumann's secretary. (*Chicago Daily News* negatives collection, DN-078750. Courtesy of the Chicago Historical Society.)

Isabelle Pope on the stand at the trial. (*Chicago Daily News* negatives collection, DN-078715. Courtesy of the Chicago Historical Society.)

William Darling Shepherd. (*Chicago Daily News* negatives collection, DN-079282. Courtesy of the Chicago Historical Society.)

William Nelson McClintock. (Courtesy of the family of Isabelle Pope.)

Billy McClintock and Isabelle Pope. He is wearing what she called his "funny, hectic socks." (Courtesy of the family of Isabelle Pope.)

Chapter 6

Defending Darl Shepherd

They may have been none too energetic, even a bit lazy.
—William Shepherd's defense attorneys, commenting
on the Shepherds

As the Shepherd trial came to a close, a University of California–Berkeley student and a vacuum cleaner salesman concocted a plan to get rich by using both the Leopold-Loeb and Shepherd cases. In a plot "too good for fiction," twenty-three-year-old Bliss Baker and C. Russell Crawford lured a society matron from her home, then called her wealthy husband to demand $50,000 for her ransom, threatening to inject the wife with disease germs if he did not comply.

The boys never had the woman and had no intentions of kidnapping her. Their hope was that the husband would pay up before she returned home, but he called the police instead and they arrested Baker at the drop site. Baker and Crawford pleaded guilty to attempted extortion and got sentences of one to two and a half years in San Quentin Prison.[1]

Back in the courtroom, Stewart and O'Brien got right down to business in what would be a very short defense case, entirely omitting an opening statement. Their case was to be built around four premises:

1. All the witnesses connecting Shepherd to typhoid germs—especially Charles Faiman—were lying.
2. Even if Faiman had supplied Shepherd with germs in 1923, those germs would have been dead by 1924.
3. Shepherd would not have had the knowledge to keep typhoid germs alive for a year.
4. There was a typhoid epidemic in Cook County at the time and more people than usual contracted it.[2]

Their final witness would be Shepherd himself, despite his extreme reluctance and Julie's opposition (she was afraid that he might "weaken under the strain of Mr. Crowe's sharp tongue" after spending three months in jail). But Darl had not testified at the inquest—in fact, he had literally run from the courtroom—and the defense attorneys knew that this would count against him if he did not take the stand at his trial.

A defendant never has to testify, of course, and juries are instructed not to look on this negatively in discussing the merits of the case. But, in reality, jurors are thinking, "If you've got a story to tell, let's hear it. We want to know how you respond to some of this testimony against you." So Darl would have to overcome his nervousness and take the stand.

Before that, Stewart and O'Brien produced two secretaries who worked in the law office where Shepherd occasionally practiced and where he had supposedly met with John P. Marchand (one of these was eighteen-year-old Eva Peterson, who was possibly Carl Sigfrid's niece). Both women said that no such individual had ever come into the office, but both admitted on cross-examination that Shepherd often remained behind when they went to lunch.[3]

The man the defense considered its biggest weapon actually bolstered the testimony given by Faiman and caused many spectators to look at that testimony in a more positive light. Dr. Frederick O. Tonney, director of the city laboratory where Faiman claimed to have received the vials of typhoid germs, was a genial, talkative man who seemed to view his questioners as students in a lecture hall where he was demonstrating.[4] He emphasized two points: keeping germs alive was very difficult to do without a lot of training, and nobody could get germs from his lab without authorization.

On cross-examination, Crowe—playing the part of a humble layman who wanted to know more about the subject—asked Dr. Tonney if he would demonstrate the method of keeping germs alive, which involved transferring them from one vial to another. The amiable doctor obliged, lecturing all the while ("you would have to have a quiet place to work in, free from air currents" and "by the way, you do it without talking, so you do not get any mouth spray on it"—this last when Crowe was about to say something).

Dr. Tonney showed how a needle could be sterilized over a Bunsen burner, and then he stuck it into the old vial, drew out the germs, and placed them into the new vial with fresh culture. That was it! Some care needed to be taken with handling the vials during the transfer and not touching the needle against the side of either vial, but once the transfer was completed and the stoppers replaced on the new vials, they could be handled in any way. They were then best preserved by being put into refrigeration.

While Dr. Tonney was saying how hard it was for someone without expertise to do this, the actual demonstration—which took only a couple of minutes—illustrated how easy it really was:

> Crowe: This is the thing you said this morning was rather a difficult technical proposition that required great learning and skill and you did not think … a druggist … would be able to do that very well.
> Tonney: I didn't say quite that, but I still say it requires practice and that the novice usually fails.
> Crowe: Well, as a matter of fact, doctor, it took you longer to tell us about it than it did for you to actually do it.
> Tonney: It does not take long to do it.

The reporter covering the trial for the *Chicago Tribune* commented that it was "something any 10-year-old could do as well."[5]

Dr. Tonney went on to say that some germ cultures could last as long as thirty years (with reculturing) and that he had known of some that had lasted six months without transference to another culture.

As far as Faiman's getting germs from the city lab was concerned, Dr. Tonney admitted that some of his employees had seen Faiman around there quite a bit. One of these, Winfield

Scott Hoerger, was listed as "Director of Laboratories" at National University. What was Hoerger's job at the city lab? He was in charge of handing out germs.

Dr. Charles Fischer, who had once employed Charles Faiman to work in his laboratory, gave the same testimony that Dr. Tonney had: that germs given to Shepherd in 1923 would be dead by 1924 because a layman could not have kept them alive. But Tonney's demonstration had ruined that line for the defense. (Fischer was also asked what Faiman's reputation for honesty was, and instead of answering "good" or "bad," as directed, said, "He is the reincarnation of Baron Munchausen.")[6]

One of Billy's nurses, Mabel McClanahan, said that Billy had told her he thought he had typhoid, which would corroborate Shepherd. But McClanahan, in a previous sworn statement, said she thought Billy had the flu and never mentioned typhoid either to his two doctors while he was still alive or to the authorities when his death was being investigated.[7] Another thing that called her current statement into question was the fact that, at the time of the investigation, much was made in the press about Shepherd's statements to Isabelle Pope and the Northern Trust about what Billy said, and she never came forward at that time to say, "Yes, Billy told me that, too."

Miss McClanahan was also asked about what she observed regarding the relations between the Shepherds and Isabelle Pope, and she related having seen Isabelle and Julie in prayer together during that time. They all seemed to get along very well, she thought.

Dr. Louis Bundesen, the health commissioner, was called to testify about the epidemic issue, and this, too, ended up undermining the defense's claim.[8] Dr. Bundesen said that most typhoid cases occurred in the fall months because of people's carelessness with water during their vacations. Oysters, too, caused typhoid, but out of 100,000 portions of oysters (all consumed) in a shipment supposed to be infected with typhoid, only 100 people got the disease.

The oysters served at the Windermere House did not cause typhoid in any other patron until three weeks after Billy's death— which means that any infected shellfish probably came in a batch subsequent to the one served to Billy's party on November 3.

As for an epidemic, there were 475 cases of typhoid in 1923. But in 1924, the year Billy contracted it, there were only 123 cases. So no special epidemic existed at that time.

Dr. Bundesen admitted that he had had to dismiss around 100 employees for rules violations and that Winfield Scott Hoerger, Faiman's colleague, was frequently called on the carpet for these. (Perhaps the fact that he was an alderman's nephew kept him from losing his job.) He once asked Hoerger how he could teach bacteriology at National University with no education or training in the subject, and Hoerger responded that the students had no idea their instructor was ignorant.

Dr. Bundesen also admitted that he had seen Charles Faiman around the Department of Health, visiting Alvira Armstrong, who used to work the counter there. Tired of the flirting and waste of time, Bundesen took Miss Armstrong off the counter and put her in an area behind a screen so Faiman couldn't see her.

In fact, Dr. Bundesen testified, Faiman had a hospital "on paper" only because someone—not necessarily Hoerger or Armstrong—violated the rules. When an inspector went to investigate, he found no patients and no hospital.

So there was no epidemic; Faiman could have gotten the germs as he had said; and keeping the germs alive was not too challenging, especially for a man with a lifelong interest in chemistry and drugs. On these technical issues, the defense clearly lost.

Several witnesses were brought forward to testify to Faiman's character, all of whom said it was bad. Besides Dr. Fischer (who was then associated with a Class C medical school, only slightly higher in reputation than National University), there was Luella Rhuebell, something of a lowlife herself, who also brought out the fact that her paycheck from Faiman had bounced.[9]

Rhuebell was asked about the famous letter Shepherd had written to the school, and the former business manager said she had never seen such a thing, nor had she seen Shepherd around the school. At one time she went through all the files, she claimed, to clean out the "dead wood" and ended up throwing out a bunch of old letters. Shepherd's wasn't there.

Of course it wasn't there! Rhuebell only worked for National University from September to December 1924, and by that time Shepherd had bought back his letter for $50. And she wouldn't have seen him around the school because by then he and Faiman were meeting at various hotels around the city.

Another "character" witness was a friend of Dr. Bristol, the one who was currently serving a term at Leavenworth for selling drugs he had bought from Faiman.[10]

Although certainly Charles Faiman was not the soul of integrity, the character witnesses brought forth by the defense were little better in that department themselves.

The last witness on that day finished up at 4:30 p.m., and Judge Lynch called a recess until the next morning, when William Darling Shepherd would finally tell his own story. His attorneys spent hours preparing him for the ordeal and bucking him up, telling him what they would ask and coaching him as to what the cross-examination would probably be like.

The next morning the courtroom was packed with people who were anxious to see Crowe make mincemeat of Darl Shepherd. The state's attorney had turned the defense's expert witnesses into prosecution witnesses. What might he do to "the panhandler"?

There is no byline to the newspaper article about Shepherd's testimony, but the style is that of Genevieve Forbes Herrick. The reporter, whoever he or she is, could find nothing at all prepossessing in the appearance or performance of the man on trial. Calling him a "pasty, pouchy, soggy man" who gave "sagging answers in a hopeless monotone," she describes him thus for her readers:

> [A] bag of a man, a loose blue bag, a sagging slack in his trousers, a sag in his jowls, pouches under his eyes; a bag of a man who shambled to the witness chair ... whose mouth is drooping dejectedly for lack of slightest resolution, whose eyes are of an unclassified, characterless blue and whose color is paste.[11]

Shepherd's answers were given in a low, droning voice that was difficult to hear. The jurors farthest away from the witness chair sat on the edges of their own chairs and strained to make out what he was saying, and Stewart frequently asked him to speak up. When asked outright on direct examination whether he had killed Billy McClintock by any means, he answered in the same droning voice. No outrage, no emphasis, no indignation—just a leaden "No, I did not."[12]

Other questions asked were whether he knew Faiman or Marchand before his arrest and whether he had ever written a letter to National University. That was it for direct examination, which had taken all of three minutes. Now it would be Crowe's turn to tear him apart.

But Crowe did not, thereby disappointing all the spectators and all those who read reports of the trial. What he did was take Shepherd through his vagabond life, letting the jury see what kind of man this was: "Shepherd the panhandler, Shepherd the soggy, hopeless ne'er-do-well who wanted a soft sitting without effort." There were no questions concerning Faiman or Marchand or his statements as to what Billy had said about having typhoid.

What Crowe did do, however, was to prove Shepherd a liar. Darl denied he had a home laboratory, despite at least two people testifying that they had seen one. He denied telling anyone that Alexander F. Reichmann had talked about getting "a slice of the estate" or that Reichmann had ever made the statement, even though several people had heard Shepherd say that he had.

Shepherd could not remember any wages he ever received for any job he had ever held (possibly they weren't very memorable). He couldn't even remember what income he took in from his law practice in 1923 (on which he paid a total tax of $4). Crowe produced some sworn testimony from the probate court during one of the Shepherds' fights with Reichmann over Billy's guardianship in 1910 that directly contradicted answers he had just given during his trial.

Shepherd had said, on cross-examination, that he had not gotten paid anything by Emma McClintock but had, instead, paid her $50 a month room and board for himself and Julie. Of course, what he was trying to do was counteract the portrait of himself as a panhandler that the prosecution had been giving out, but his statement was a lie. In his 1910 testimony in probate court he said Emma had paid him about $200 a month to be her chauffeur and perform other tasks for her, and he never mentioned anything about his paying room and board.

Crowe continually boxed Shepherd into a corner by asking, "Do you recall this testimony at the hearing in the probate court?" and would read him the question and then Shepherd's answer. If it didn't hurt him, Darl would recall it. But for most of these his response was, "I recall neither the question nor the answer." Over the issue of whether he paid Emma or got paid by her, Crowe exposed him so badly that silence was his only response for several questions.

Shepherd was literal in his answers. Asked if he had told a man named Watt that he was going to "build an estate down in Florida and go and live there," he said, "I did not." But it turned out he had told Watt he was building a *cottage* down there—not an estate. Asked if he was going to request that Billy give him a piece of property on Michigan Avenue, he replied that Billy didn't own anything on Michigan Avenue. After further questioning it was revealed that Darl had, indeed, made that statement to someone, but the property turned out to be on South Water Street instead—not Michigan Avenue.

There were a few questions about the will ("Didn't you know it's unethical to draw up a will when you're the beneficiary?"), and then the cross-examination was over. The courtroom was stunned when Crowe announced he had no more questions. Darl Shepherd was relieved and let out an audible sigh when he got back to the defense table. He had gotten off easy and he knew it.

The order of closing arguments would be Gorman first and Crowe last for the state, with Stewart and O'Brien sandwiched in between. George Gorman focused on the panhandler issue and also pointed out that one constant in Shepherd's life had been his connection with drugs and chemistry—his hobbies, so to speak.[13] He was not the layman his attorneys tried to present, an inexperienced bungler who could not have kept typhoid germs alive for a year.

Gorman included Julie Shepherd in his accusations, and she cried throughout much of his closing argument. She was consoled by a much younger Elsie Gunn, Rev. Carl Naumann's secretary, who accompanied Julie to court each day. Did the Shepherds love Billy? Gorman concluded:

Sure, they loved him—as a tramp loves a meal ticket ... as a farmer loves his hogs. The farmer will take good care of a sick pig. He will develop him and bring him to the point where he is ready for slaughter.

Even Rev. Naumann was included in the plot to get Billy's money for the Shepherds. His part was to goad Billy into doing something good for the two people who had brought him up, by playing on his guilt and saying it was the young man's duty to provide generously for them.

The character witnesses had said Faiman couldn't be believed. But, Gorman pointed out, Faiman called himself a murderer and incriminated himself in the plot. Why would he do this if it were not the truth?

While Julie Shepherd cried during Gorman's closing argument, Darl just looked straight ahead, exhibiting no reaction to what was being said about him or his wife.

When it was the two defense attorneys' turn to speak, they didn't present Shepherd's case, but instead chose to attack witnesses against him.[14] Stewart accused Reichmann and Olson of master-minding the plot to divest Shepherd of the McClintock estate. He called Faiman "a dirty, dangerous, deceitful little rat":

> If you believe Faiman—If you believe that Shepherd went out to consult with him about germs, then I say to you—hang Shepherd! If you believe that Shepherd murdered an innocent youth—hang him! Hanging would be too good for him.

When Shepherd heard his own attorney yell "Hang him!" he jumped to attention.[15]

W. W. O'Brien accused Crowe of going along with Olson in prosecuting Shepherd in a groundless case and insinuated that Isabelle Pope was not so innocent, either, in her insistence on marrying an unconscious dying man. In his scathing denunciation of Faiman, who was somewhat effeminate in appearance and manner, he referred to him as "a perfect lady." (Witnesses usually come in one of two flavors, he said: male or female. But which was Faiman?) He said that Faiman and Rongetti should do a vaudeville act together. O'Brien closed out his argument by asking the jury to return a "not guilty" verdict in record time.

State's Attorney Robert Crowe's closing was disappointing and also shorter than expected.[16] (Attorneys prided themselves on speaking for hours at closing argument.) He spent most of it criticizing the unethical behavior of the defense attorneys in attacking upstanding members of the bar and calling them liars and thieves and murderers for concocting a wild plot to send an innocent man to the gallows:

> I think that is a mighty serious accusation to be made in any court of justice. I would expect charges of that sort to be made in barrooms but not in a court of justice by officers of the court, unless there was evidence upon which to base those charges ... charges that the most prominent and influential lawyers in this city, public officials holding powerful positions and a big financial institution [the Northern Trust] had all conspired for the purpose of committing murder ... under the guise of justice, in order that some heirs that nobody knows, living in the western states, may inherit his property.

This was their entire defense, Crowe pointed out. Moreover, their client had been proved a liar out of his own mouth. He concluded by asking for the death penalty.

When the jury retired at 3:47 p.m. to deliberate, an immediate vote was taken to see where everyone was in their thinking.[17] (There seems to have been eavesdropping at the door, as the newspapers were privy to parts of the discussion that were "overheard," and a New York newspaper had an issue out announcing the verdict before the jurors even got back to the courtroom.) The first vote was split: seven jurors for "guilty" and five for "not guilty." Some of the jurors who voted not guilty said they believed Shepherd *was*, in fact, guilty but thought there was a reasonable doubt as to where Billy had picked up typhoid.

Six ballots were taken before a unanimous verdict was reached (required in a criminal trial). The lone holdout, until the end, was juror Mark Spikens, who was impressed by Dr. Bundesen's statement that only one oyster in a thousand might contain typhoid germs, which to him meant that Billy had probably not gotten infected that way. Spikens thought Shepherd should get the minimum sentence of fourteen years in prison, but eventually he was swayed to vote with the others, and at 10:07 p.m. the bailiff was told they had reached a verdict.

Before letting the jury back into the courtroom, however, Judge Lynch had the bailiff get the courtroom back into a semblance of order: spectators and reporters had made themselves at home, lounging on desks, smoking, eating lunch, and discarding litter on the floor. The bailiff also warned against any demonstrations or disorder when the verdict was read.[18]

It did no good. Word of the "not guilty" verdict had already leaked into the courtroom, and photographers' flashbulbs were popping before it was officially read. Photographers leaped onto chairs, the rail of the jury box, and the clerk's desk to get shots of Shepherd and his attorneys ("Get him in front"; "Get out of the way, Jim"; "For the love of Mike, give me a chance"; "That's it, just a minute, hold it!"), and there was so much smoke from the flashbulbs that it was difficult to see anyone. Chairs were overturned and "everybody in the room was dusted with the fine ash of the flashlight powder." Women screamed in terror at the heat, the smoke, the pushing and shoving, and the general pandemonium. Some had their dresses nearly ripped off in the melee. Shepherd clung to one of his attorneys, grinning his loopy grin. Sitting high over the courtroom, Judge Lynch threw back his head and laughed at the commotion below.[19]

Elsie Gunn was there, and so was Eva Peterson. Both rushed up to throw their arms around Shepherd in congratulations. (Julie had chosen to wait out the verdict in a local hotel because she didn't want to hear Crowe's closing argument, no doubt assuming it would contain more of the "panhandling" accusations of his opening.) Darl went around shaking hands with the jurors, the judge, and the reporters. Then he went to join his wife at the hotel.[20] Soon, the murder charge against him for the death of Billy's mother would also be dropped, mostly because of jurisdictional problems in that the poisoning had taken place in Texas.[21] (However, the death took place in Illinois, so they really could have gone ahead with it if they had chosen to do so.)

A *New York Times* editorial criticized the uncivilized courtroom behavior when the Shepherd verdict was read and asked the American Bar Association to do something about a growing trend in that vein. Judges should take better charge of their courtrooms and punish offenders as an example to others, the *Times* argued. The editorial paired the Shepherd example with that of another recent mob scene at a British golf championship. Apparently, the crowd had become so unruly that the police were unable to keep them off the greens while the contestants were playing. One golfer was bitten by a spectator's dog and others had their golf balls kicked around.[22]

In Indianapolis, Darl Shepherd's seventy-seven-year-old mother was overjoyed at her son's acquittal, but not surprised by it. After all, she said, the spirits had appeared to her and told her he would be acquitted. Her husband, Benjamin, a member with her in the Spiritualist Church, declared that a couple of days before the verdict they had received a message signed by none other than former president Benjamin Harrison: "You see, that is Mrs. Hayden's second cousin [her maiden name was Harrison]," explained Hayden. "He told us that we had no cause to worry at all."[23]

Martha Hayden's son's primer-prose reaction fit his bland personality:

I do not know what to say. I am going home. I am going home after three months and thirteen days. I was arrested on Friday the 13th and I am leaving my cell, which is No. 13, on a Friday.[24]

Stewart's response to the acquittal was that it was in actuality a verdict of "guilty" against those evil plotters who had set Shepherd up in an attempt to get the McClintock money.[25]

When Rev. Carl Naumann heard the news, he asked, "Is it true?" then went on to say that justice had triumphed and God had been merciful to his persecuted friend. Did he pray for Shepherd's acquittal? No, he had prayed for the truth to come out instead: "If I had supposed Shepherd was guilty I would have asked permission of Sheriff Hoffman to stay down there at the county jail and wring the confession from him. All honor to Stewart, but to God the glory."[26]

And what of Charles Faiman, still in jail on the McClintock murder charge? Although Darl Shepherd, the man he supposedly conspired with, had been acquitted and set free, Faiman was kept in jail for three more days before the murder charge against him was stricken "with leave to reinstate." Apparently, the state was contemplating filing perjury charges against him. Although they could never re-try Shepherd under the double jeopardy clause, the "leave to reinstate" against Faiman meant they could at least get one of the conspirators sometime in the future if more evidence were found.

Faiman was philosophical about the acquittal: "I told the truth and eased my conscience, and that is all," he told reporters. "It rather eases a fellow's mind to know that he has done his duty. I told the truth despite the consequences." At first he couldn't believe he was free. When it dawned on him that he could go, he ran down the stairs, ran to his home, and—soon after that— ran from the state of Illinois.[27]

Robert Crowe was likewise philosophical, saying that the state had done its best and he was already focusing on his next case— which may be somewhat revealing as to how Crowe approached the Shepherd trial.[28] Unsurprisingly, Judge Harry Olson was steamed about the way the prosecution had fumbled what he saw as a winnable case. The state had not cooperated with him, he claimed (which, for Harry Olson, probably meant they had not let him take charge), and had not presented all the competent evidence available.[29]

For example, why no evidence of Emma McClintock's murder? Where were Fosberg, White, and Kles? Where was Faiman's letter ordering a $100,000 school? (Crowe had even promised in his opening statement that the architect contacted by Faiman for the new school would testify, but he was never called.)[30] Why wasn't Judge Olson allowed to bring out more information on the stand? Why wasn't Shepherd cross-examined on the events surrounding Billy's death?

Crowe's response to Judge Olson's criticism was barely civil: "I do not wish to enter into a controversy with a man in Chief Justice Olson's mental condition." Yet he did go on to defend some of his omissions: Robert White, with his change in testimony, then back again, coupled with his disappearing act, destroyed his own credibility. (This was probably true.) Louis Kles had a grudge against his employer, Shepherd, and Crowe was afraid this would lessen his testimony. But it would have substantiated statements made by other employees. The dates Dr. Fosberg gave for meeting with Shepherd coincided with times when Shepherd was in Arizona. (But Fosberg could have been mistaken about the dates—this was no reason to exclude him.)[31]

Though he did not say it, Crowe may have been influenced by rumors—started by the defense—that Fosberg was involved with abortions, and by Clarence Darrow's statement that the doctor had offered to testify for the defense, for a fee, at the Leopold-Loeb hearing.[32] Darrow did not use him and never revealed what the nature of his testimony was to be, but the insinuation was that Fosberg was willing to be a "hired gun" for the highest bidder.

As for the cross-examination of Shepherd, he was a liar, Crowe said. It would hurt the prosecution to ask a stream of questions that he would simply deny. (Defendants do this all the time. How would it hurt the prosecution?)

Although Shepherd did deny everything surrounding his connection with Faiman and Marchand, there were some things he admitted that it seems he could have been tripped up on. The most glaring one is his statement to at least two people that Billy had told him he thought he had typhoid. Crowe did an excellent job of backing him into a corner over the payment vs. room-and-board issue, and he could surely have done the same with this: When did Billy tell you this? Yet you let him continue to go out at night as usual? Why didn't you say anything to the doctor? If you thought he had typhoid, why did you give him a laxative? If you didn't think he had typhoid, despite his statement, why bring it up at all before the diagnosis?

But, of course, the biggest mistake, the one that sank the ship of the state, was the disowning of Charles Faiman. Had Crowe stuck by him as his own witness, the verdict might have gone the other way, particularly on the heels of the testimony of Dr. Tonney, whose demonstration showed how essentially simple a thing the reculturation of germs is. It is evident that the jury chose not to believe Faiman, and therefore there was no real connection between Shepherd and typhoid germs. They thought Billy could have picked up the germs anywhere: hence, reasonable doubt as to Shepherd's involvement.

After the trial, Mark Spikens, the holdout juror, told reporters that the state "did not present sufficient evidence." Another juror specifically pointed to the state's refusal to vouch for Faiman as the reason for the verdict: "I don't see how the jury could be expected to believe him [after that]," he commented.[33]

It had probably been a mistake for Robert Crowe to take over the prosecution of Shepherd so close on the heels of his pull-out-all-the-stops involvement in the Leopold-Loeb case. He had seen the latter as the case that would insure his re-election in the fall of 1924[34]—which it had done—but with the Shepherd trial he must have felt that he had been suckered into something whose evidence turned out, in the end, to be evanescent and insubstantial. Crowe's effort here was less than his best. *New York Times* reporter Russell Owen commented that "[the state's attorney's] heart wasn't in it."[35]

An editorial in the *Waukesha [Wisconsin] Daily Freeman* just put it off to the usual form of justice in Chicago: "[A] lot of real murderers in Chicago have not been found guilty, and besides thousands have attempted to honor them at their graves. But such is the community of Chicago."[36]

William Darling Shepherd, back home and bolder on his own turf, said he would be suing the "conspirators" (Judge Olson, Alexander Reichmann, and John H. S. Lee) for slander and false imprisonment. Any money he got from the suit would go to charity, as he just wanted to punish the plotters.[37] Needless to say, neither the suit nor the gift to charity ever took place.

Nor did Shepherd ever repay the $50,000 loan to the Toombs & Daily brokerage firm.[38] Were his attorneys, Stewart and O'Brien, paid? Although nothing was revealed about this, the answer may be discerned in their refusal to represent him in his upcoming will contest, despite their having said earlier that they would do so.

A vital question remains in this sad affair, one that was not solved by the verdict: was Billy McClintock murdered?

Chapter 7

Was It Oysters or Murder?

To beguile the time,
Look like the time, bear welcome in your eye,
Your hand, your tongue. Look like the innocent flower
But be the serpent under't ...
Leave all the rest to me.
       —Lady Macbeth to Macbeth, *Macbeth*, act I, scene V,
                  64–67, 75

In September 1984 approximately 1,000 people in the small town of The Dalles, Oregon, and neighboring communities were sickened by a mild form of the typhoid virus, *Salmonella typhimurium*, which had been put on items in several restaurant salad bars by a religious cult called the Rajneeshees. Aggressive disciples of their leader, the Bhagwan Shree Rajneesh, their goal was to take over the county in the local elections and turn it into their own private domain. The poisoning of the salad bars was payback in an ongoing war between locals and cult members, and a means of preventing people from going to the polls in November. The September incident was a trial run.[1]

The original plan was to use *Salmonella typhi*, which causes typhoid fever and would have been fatal to most people. Indeed, the Rajneeshees had these germs ready for distribution, but a cooler head among them said that a typhoid outbreak would cause the bacteria purchase to be traced back to them.

How had the Rajneeshees gotten typhoid germs? In much the same way that Charles Faiman had done so: by claiming to be a legitimate medical facility. A nurse who was a cult member established the Rajneesh Medical Corporation, and so was able to purchase bacteria cultures from both VWR Scientific in Seattle and a germ bank in Virginia called American Type Culture Collection (ATCC). The typhoid germs were ordered from ATCC. After that, "growing germs was easy; the process was like brewing beer."[2]

If it was possible for ordinary citizens to obtain disease germs in 1984, it was certainly possible for them to do so in 1924, when such things were less restricted. No one was ever able to contradict Faiman's claim that he had gotten bacteria cultures from Chicago's medical laboratory, and the evidence showed that he probably did so. Dr. Tonney demonstrated how easy it was to transfer the germs to a new culture, and so keep them alive until needed. Shepherd's background not only included extensive scientific experience, but—if Faiman is to be believed—he was thoroughly coached in the culture of bacteria and their transfer to Billy's drinking water.

So the procuring and cultivating of typhoid germs, and their infecting of Billy, were entirely possible. The problem the jury in the Shepherd case had was the lack of evidence connecting the defendant to the typhoid germs, which meant that Faiman's testimony was not believed. What could today's technology have told us about the truth of what happened to Billy McClintock if it had been available back in 1924?

DNA

All living things have deoxyribonucleic acid, or DNA, the bar code of life that records all the characteristics of that organism. This applies to bacteria just as it does to humans, so it would have been possible to isolate the DNA of the typhoid germs found in Billy McClintock and compare them to any such germs found in the batch of oysters served at the Windermere House. If the DNA matched, then the typhoid came from there. If it did not, then the source of the typhoid was elsewhere. And that "elsewhere" could have been anything and not necessarily germs supplied by Darl Shepherd. So a match with the Windermere oysters would exonerate him, but a mismatch would not definitely prove that he was guilty.

However, the Windermere reported that there were no other cases of typhoid in its patrons until three weeks after Billy's death, which would put the tainted batch at the hotel a month after Billy ate oysters there. Even if there had been typhoid-infected oysters when Billy was at the Windermere, that batch would not have been available by the time poisoning was suspected in late December. Thus, DNA would have been helpful, but not definitive.

TELEPHONE RECORDS

Charles Faiman claimed that he and Shepherd had exchanged telephone calls during and after Billy's illness. Shepherd said he had never heard of or met Faiman before his entry into the case. Today's technology would enable investigators to retrieve the phone records of both men and determine whether either had placed calls to the other, and when. If such calls had been made, it would prove Shepherd a liar and tend to support Faiman's testimony against him.

POLYGRAPH TESTS

The lie detector was new back in 1925; it is still not consistently reliable enough for a subject's failing score to be admitted in court. The polygraph measures changes in galvanic skin response, respiration, blood pressure, and pulse rate. However, in order to work at its optimum, the system needs a competent operator and a subject who is not under the influence of one or more of the following variables: medication or other drugs; alcohol; paralysis; hunger; cold, flu, or other respiratory ailment; heart trouble; pregnancy; emotional instability; mental illness; recent surgery; low mental ability; and lack of feelings of guilt.[3]

William Darling Shepherd had been a chronic liar his whole life, so unless he had feelings of guilt or fear during a polygraph test, he would probably pass it. Lying came easily to him. If, on the other hand, he felt the machine could catch him in a lie and he feared the outcome if discovered, then he would have exhibited the predicted physiological responses to questions regarding Billy's death. In that case, he would fail it.

Likewise, Charles Faiman was an accomplished liar. His polygraph would show either that he was telling the truth about his interaction with Shepherd or that he was calm and composed while telling lies. In either case, he would undoubtedly get a passing score. However, it is possible that the lie detector might have worked better with other players in the drama, such as Marchand, Fosberg, and Breidigan.

OTHER MODERN TECHNOLOGY

Since Billy's death was not a bloody one produced by gunshot wounds or blunt force trauma, blood pattern analysis and other such tests would not be helpful. Nor would trace evidence or fingerprinting, as the suspects—the Shepherds—lived with the victim and would naturally leave their fibers and prints around the home.

Therefore, the only definitive modern forensic tool would be the phone records.

THE 1925 CRIMINAL INVESTIGATION

The police did a terrible job of investigating the Shepherds, possibly because of their somewhat upper-class status, albeit a status established on the coattails of the McClintocks. The biggest oversight was their failure to search the house for the laboratory that so many servants claimed William Shepherd kept there. Just finding the lab itself would be incriminating, but they also might have turned up typhoid or other bacteria cultures. On the other hand, Shepherd's imminent arrest was hardly a secret, and it may be that he took pains to dispose of all items in the laboratory.

There is no indication that either of the Shepherds was subject to police interrogation once they were in custody. Darl Shepherd was so weak-willed that he might have given the whole game away if approached correctly.

THE WITNESSES

Those who have been in law enforcement a long time say they don't believe in coincidences:[4] if many pieces of evidence point to someone's guilt, then it is far more likely that person is guilty and not the victim of some outlandishly cruel twist of fate or an evil conspiracy. Perhaps this is a cynical view of the world, but it is a maxim that proves true almost all the time: "Coincidence is the messenger of truth."[5]

If we take all the witnesses who said that Shepherd had a laboratory in his home—at least three of the servants (Anna Anderson, Stella Costigan, and Louis Kles)—and those who claimed that he had sought out information about typhoid cultures (Fosberg, Breidigan, Faiman, Marchand, and White), it adds up to very incriminating testimony. What are the odds that all of these people from varying backgrounds got together to cooperate in some kind of conspiracy against the Shepherds to prevent them from inheriting Billy's money? If conspiracy there were, it would seem that at least one of the participants would have leaked it at some point. None did.

JUDGE HARRY OLSON

The entire investigation into Billy's death was the result of an anonymous letter that Judge Olson said he received shortly after the funeral. Supposedly, this letter said that Billy was probably poisoned. But it is more likely that there was no such letter (it was never produced, and once the investigation gained steam, he stopped referring to it) and that Olson used this as a ploy to force an inquiry in a way that wouldn't make it seem to be coming from him. One of Billy's relatives, Maude Walker, did write and ask Olson what Billy died of, but there was no suspicion of foul play in her letter and she didn't withhold her name.[6]

Olson had been distrustful of the Shepherds since Emma McClintock's death, and he also knew that his brother, Dr. Oscar, had counseled Billy to separate himself from them when he turned twenty-one. The judge was suspicious of Emma's strange death and hurry-up burial, and when Billy died so suddenly, Olson undoubtedly wanted someone in authority to take a closer look. If Olson had an anonymous letter and an investigation proved the Shepherds innocent, then he would be protected in the event of a defamation-of-character charge.

Judge Olson claimed that, after Billy's death, which aroused his suspicions, he called up two reporters and told them to ask Shepherd about the contents of the will. These were the two who got different stories—both erroneous—about the disposition of the estate. Olson felt this was further proof of Shepherd's guilt.[7]

CHARLES FAIMAN

Charles Faiman was a reluctant witness. He never came forward on his own, but only when dragged in by the (also reluctant) testimony of his colleague John Marchand about the letter written by Shepherd. At first Faiman even tried to protect Shepherd by pretending he didn't know him and knew nothing about a letter inquiring about bacteriology lessons. Even after he was threatened with violence by Marchand, his information came sporadically: First he said the vials were missing after Shepherd had been there one time. Then he said he had given Shepherd the germs because he asked for them. Finally, he implicated himself in the plot to kill Billy McClintock. This timeline works against a theory of conspiracy against Darl Shepherd because if there had been one, Faiman would have come forward immediately to fulfill his role.

Faiman was a con artist and a practiced liar, but he had nothing to gain and everything to lose by implicating Shepherd in this plot. If Shepherd were convicted, so, too, would Faiman be. His career as a "doctor" and head of National University was over no matter what the outcome, as his testimony exposed both his own fake credentials and those of his school. The defense made much of Faiman's reputation, but when someone like Shepherd makes a deal with the devil, there won't be angels as witnesses to the transaction.

Therefore, Charles Faiman must have been telling the truth about Shepherd's plan to kill Billy McClintock. He may have gilded over his own role in it, making it more passive than it actually was, but it must be assumed that he presented Shepherd's part accurately.

WILLIAM DARLING SHEPHERD

Darl and Julie had a very cushy lifestyle going for themselves at the McClintock home. Instead of having to drift here and there looking for jobs and sustenance, they could live off the estate left by the late William McClintock Sr. However, something happened in 1909, two years after McClintock's death, to threaten this situation. It is entirely possible that Emma McClintock was at the end of her rope with these two—or maybe just with Darl—and was giving off hints that they would be sent packing. When she went down to Bay View, Texas, to see about the progress on the cottage and why the bills weren't being paid with the money she had given Darl Shepherd, she might have indicated that she was not best pleased with him.

It would have been incredibly easy for Shepherd, who carried around a veritable drugstore, to have slipped some shavings from a bichloride of mercury tablet into Emma's food or water. Then, when she became ill, she would have gladly accepted any nostrums offered by the former druggist. Witnesses in Texas said they saw him give her medicine, and Emma herself told Stella Costigan that Shepherd had given her drugs on other occasions.

Once the Shepherds were in charge of Billy, did Darl—alone or with his wife—plan to kill him? Probably not. No sense in killing the goose that laid the golden egg unless there was no other way to attain the gold. While Billy was under their control and they had access to the estate, even though that access was limited, there would have been no need for such a plan.

When Billy was dying, the houseman and chauffeur Louis Kles said he was sent on all sorts of errands, but never for Billy's medicine. He was told by Julie that "Mr. Shepherd will get the prescriptions filled," but Kles said this was never done at the Kenilworth pharmacy. Later, Shepherd asked Kles to tell the druggist at that pharmacy that Dr. Stolp told Shepherd to go to the Wilmette pharmacy to get the prescriptions filled. When Darl and Julie were leaving for New Mexico, Shepherd pleaded with Kles: "Please, Louie, don't mention anything about Billy. If everything comes out all right, I'll fix you up."[8] Kles also claimed that Darl had promised him $10,000 if he kept his mouth shut.[9]

However, when Mrs. Shepherd became ill after Billy's death, Darl Shepherd went right to the Kenilworth pharmacy to get her prescription filled.[10] So, was Billy's medicine procured at all? And if not, whose idea was it not to get it?

Here is where Darl Shepherd's psychological makeup comes in. There is nothing in his background to indicate that he would have committed violence in order to get money. Would he lie for it? Absolutely. Charles Faiman was not the only "reincarnation of Baron Munchausen" in this drama. Shepherd's own commanding officer called him the biggest liar in the company, one who would turn an encounter with a barking dog into a near-fatal attack by a raging bull. Would he cheat for it? Without doubt. Who knows what machinations he was pulling with his land deals?

But would he kill for it? This is a harder call. If the newspaper reported this correctly, then Shepherd's attorney (and former partner) Robert Stoll made a strange comment: he told a reporter that Shepherd was "broke and dependent upon McClintock and that he would be flat if the marriage took place, but that he was going to stop it."[11] It seems odd that Stoll would say this, even if true, as he continued to represent the Shepherds and was a loyal and staunch defender. It indicates that possibly Shepherd would commit murder for money if he felt desperate enough and couldn't stop the marriage any other way.

But the bulk of the evidence suggests that William Shepherd seemed content with an easy life as long as he didn't have to exert himself too much. He lived with the Bohmies until kicked out (and felt no need to dispose of any of them so he could stay), and he lived with various relatives until he married Julie Graf. He would have been content to live off Billy McClintock forever, and if it came to an end because Billy told the Shepherds to go, no doubt he would have shuffled off and found someone else to take them in—probably his mother and his stepfather, who were still living in Indianapolis.

Moreover, the McClintock typhoid scheme seems far beyond both the imagination and the energy level of Darl Shepherd. He could be a gofer, carrying out plans devised by others, but for the real brains behind the scheme, we will have to look elsewhere.

JULIA GRAF SHEPHERD

Julie Shepherd was cut from entirely different cloth than was her husband. Where he was listless and laid-back, she was frenetic and ambitious. While Darl was happy just to have a roof over his head and meals provided for him, Julie was overwhelmed by the magnitude of her friend Emma's wealth. Her constant refrain to Anna Anderson was, "Anna, do you realize you are working for a millionaire?"[12] It seems to have dominated her consciousness at all times.

Julie was a schemer. It was undoubtedly her idea to look up the grieving widow McClintock in the first place. Once there, she manipulated Emma, cut her off from her friends, and tyrannized her servants until she was more in charge of the household than its owner was. When Anna Anderson was in the hospital with the flu one time, Emma apologized for not having gone to visit her sooner, but every time she planned to go, Julie wanted to go along, and that meant Emma and Anna would not be able to talk.[13] Emma seems to have been incapable of exerting her own will against that of her friend.

When Emma wanted to adopt a little boy as a playmate for Billy, Julie objected so strongly that Emma dropped the issue. Why would Julie care about this? It is possible that she already had the idea of eliminating Emma McClintock and did not want the burden of raising two children. One was more than enough for her.

When Emma went down to Bay View in late May 1909, Julie would have picked up on her displeasure with Darl Shepherd. At that time, fearing for their future, she may have instructed her husband to slip something into the widow's food, if she had not already previously decided to get rid of her friend and bene-factor. When Emma became ill, Julie pressured her to name her, Julie, as Billy's guardian should anything happen.

Back in Chicago, with Emma's body not even cold, Julie removed an expensive ring from her hand, ostensibly "for Billy." But the fact that she could focus on such a material thing at that time shows both her lack of feeling for Emma McClintock and her obsession with wealth.

According to a witness at Emma's funeral, a relative suggested that an autopsy be done, but Julie strongly opposed it.[14] Some other guests voiced their opinion that Emma might have been poisoned, an idea that put Julie in a state of high dudgeon.[15] If she were innocent, why not consent to an autopsy when the death was so sudden and so strange? Why get so indignant?

Emma was not dead a month when Julie and Darl dragged Billy out to Colorado to consult with Carl Sigfrid about how to break the trust and the co-guardianship with Alexander Reichmann. If that could be done, there would be no monitoring of how much money the Shepherds received or what they spent it on.

Isabelle Pope later told her daughters that when Billy went to Dartmouth and was out of the control of the Shepherds, he began seeing that things were not right in his home and did not com-pletely trust his guardians. Isabelle did not spell out what she meant by this, but Billy became more independent in his approach to them.[16] Did he suspect they might have killed his mother? Did he suspect they might have designs on his own wealth? Probably not, but he does seem to have wanted to dissociate himself from them once he got married.

As Billy's relationship with Isabelle grew more serious and more emotionally removed from the Shepherds, Julie must have begun to panic. Perhaps she thought Billy would not provide for them after his marriage and this was why she tried so hard to prevent the engagement. She couldn't possibly have thought he would remain single forever out of loyalty to his guardians, but she did everything she could to instill in him a sense of guilt and betrayal. It is a telling fact that she asked Billy not to get engaged or married before he was twenty-one, the age when he would inherit his estate: if he got married before then, the Shepherds would have no chance at all to get it.

However, Billy might have been "allowed" to marry someone other than Isabelle Pope. Both Isabelle and Julie were women who were stronger than their mates. But, while Isabelle was a force for good in Billy's life, Julie pushed her husband down another path entirely. Julie must have seen that she would not be able to manipulate Isabelle the way she had Emma McClintock, and probably blamed the young woman for Billy's estrangement. It was all too evident to her that, after their marriage, Billy and Isabelle would have little to do with the Shepherds. There went the soft lifestyle they had counted on.

In fact, while Billy was at Dartmouth, Julie may have been testing her prospective daughter-in-law for signs of pliability. There was the issue of the bobbed hair—would she follow Julie's advice (and preference) and ignore Billy's wishes? There was also Julie's attempt to get Isabelle to change her religion from Episcopal to Lutheran, which Isabelle had absolutely no intention of doing. In a letter to Billy, she told him what Julie was trying to do:

> I am afraid she is trying to make me a Lutheran. She said that often the girl went to a different church than the boy did and that it was so hard to get a boy to go to church anyway, that if the girl did not go to his church he would not go at all. She said that she had seen it work out that if the girl did go to the boy's church he would go and all was lovely. I could not tell her that I just could not be a Lutheran, so I just said that I thought it would turn out all right. I surely hope it does. We are not going to have any trouble over which church we are going to, are we? I will go to any church (Protestant, of course) except the Lutheran. That sounds dreadfully narrow and foolish but I mean it and we might as well understand each other now. What have you to say on the subject?[17]

Isabelle did accompany the Shepherds to St. Paul's Lutheran Church one Sunday, but it was in the spirit of cooperation,[18] and she was a little afraid—as were most people—of being too firm with Julie. Julie must have realized that Isabelle exerted a strong influence over Billy, an influence that would take precedence over her own after their marriage. Had Isabelle acquiesced in the matter of religion—a very important item for most people—perhaps Julie might have let the young people get married, knowing she could continue to run Billy's life. When Isabelle failed this test, Julie would fear for Darl's and her future.

Some time in the fall of 1923, as Billy was approaching his twenty-first birthday, the plot may have been hatched, maybe not as a definite scheme, but as a backup plan in case it looked as if Billy would be leaving them out in the cold. If Julie had been the source of the idea, she would have importuned her husband to come up with something that would get rid of Billy and not be traced to them. Because of Darl's experience as a pharmacist, he might have thought of bacteria himself, possibly remembering his conversations with Dr. Breidigan long ago; or, it could be that the plot really was put into play when Billy was still a child.

There is no doubt that Julie Shepherd had the intelligence and the drive to concoct this plot. She seems cold-blooded enough for it, too. Judge Harry Olson called her Lady Macbeth, and she is certainly a better candidate for the schemer role than is her wishy-washy husband.

But there are two puzzling pieces of information that don't jibe with Julie Shepherd's being the real source of this scheme. First of all, there is Isabelle Pope's statement to Maureen McKernan that Julie seemed to be under the influence of her husband, that he had an unusual power over her.[19] Isabelle was very young, of course, and so maybe not as astute in judging others as an older and more experienced person would be; and it may be that she was interpreting things in a light that was most unfavorable to Darl Shepherd because he was the one going on trial for Billy's murder. But if the statement is accurate, it doesn't fit the profile of Julie as the one in charge; and the former maid, Anna Anderson, said that Darl exerted a lot of influence over Emma McClintock.[20]

Another strange thing is the fact that Julie never visited Darl in jail all the time he was there. If she were in charge of the plot, she would surely fear his softness, that he might cave in or, in his blabby way, say too much—either of which was entirely possible. A more natural thing would be for her to go down there and encourage him to "screw [his] courage to the sticking-place."[21]

But if Julie was not the mastermind, then who was?

CARL J. SIGFRID

The shadowy background presence of Carl Sigfrid is everywhere, a veritable motif running through the case. In his own life he was hardly the upstanding citizen he liked to present himself to be. A notorious womanizer and philanderer, he was also known as a "wheeler-dealer" in Ouray County.[22] It must be asked: why did he change his name from Siegfred Peterson? It is not as if Peterson was an unpronounceable Swedish name, so possibly he did something in Kansas that he wanted to erase by going to Colorado and starting over.

In 1907, after William McClintock died and the Shepherds arrived at Emma's door, Carl Sigfrid came from Colorado to try to talk her into letting him take over managing her husband's estate. Her refusal may have sealed her doom.

Perhaps Sigfrid was directing the Shepherds behind the scenes, telling them what to do and when. Darl Shepherd told a reporter that Sigfrid began courting Emma again after her husband died. If this was true and she was not responding to him (once bitten, twice shy), it is possible that Sigfrid was the one who told his cousin Julie that she and Darl should move in with the widow and take steps to get the Fatal Fortune, since he would not be able to.

When Emma refused to allow Sigfrid to manage her estate, he might have decided that the only way to get it was to kill her. How he must have raged when he found out that Emma had put the estate with the Northern Trust on her deathbed! After her death he summoned the Shepherds to Ouray to discuss what to do about that.

The Shepherds would have consulted him again when it looked as if Billy was pulling away from them. Sigfrid must have been hanging around the Kenilworth home enough to make it plausible that Billy would have left something to him in his will, which is what Darl Shepherd (falsely) told two reporters. Perhaps it was Sigfrid's idea for Shepherd to look into the possibility of bacterial poisoning.

Sigfrid had told the people in Ouray, Colorado, that he was related to Richard Loeb and had been summoned by the family to go to Chicago to help in his defense. But this was not true: Sigfrid had nothing to do with either the Loebs or the case. The timing is interesting here, however: Leopold and Loeb were arrested in June 1924 and their sentencing hearing began on July 23. That covers the time when Billy came home from Dartmouth to announce that he would be taking over his estate and not going back to school, and that he and Isabelle would be getting married that February—four months earlier than planned. This is also the time when he put the Kenilworth home on the market without consulting the Shepherds.

So the family who summoned Sigfrid to Chicago would have been the Shepherds, not the Loebs. Why would Sigfrid lie about why he went to Chicago? Possibly to cover his tracks in case anyone should make a connection between his visit and Billy's death; or to make himself seem more important (another Baron Munchausen!) and at the same time hide the real reason for his visit.

The Shepherds would have sensed a crisis here with Billy's behavior and wanted Sigfrid's advice. Darl Shepherd had already investigated the possibility of typhoid, and now he would have stepped up his efforts at this time. Interestingly, some associates of Charles Faiman said Faiman had come into quite a bit of money (source unknown) in August 1924.[23] Could it have come from Carl Sigfrid?

Sigfrid also arranged for some of the financing of Darl Shepherd's defense. Toombs & Daily, the brokerage firm, had invested money in an Ouray gold mine, the Jessica. As the bulk of Sigfrid's law practice involved representing gold mines, he undoubtedly represented this one and became acquainted with Roy Toombs that way. A few years after Shepherd's trial it was revealed that the $50,000 loan was never paid back, and that Toombs was guilty of spending approximately $3,000,000 of his clients' money instead of investing it. He used it to finance Shepherd and also spent it on theater tickets, women, and the Jessica gold mine.[24] Did Sigfrid profit from this?

Carl Sigfrid fits the profile of the kind of person who could have masterminded the scheme to kill Billy McClintock. He had few moral and ethical scruples. Like his cousin Julie, he was a schemer, trying to get control of Emma McClintock's estate and plotting with the Shepherds to break the trust. There is also the story of his underground tunnel, where his informants kept him up on who was doing what. Did he use this information for blackmail? For controlling others? Whatever his purpose, it could not have been benign.

Sigfrid may very well have been communicating with Darl Shepherd while he sat in jail awaiting trial, making sure that Shepherd didn't crack under the pressure. Whether he visited was never mentioned, but his presence is not always brought to the forefront. In fact, only an accidental reference in an attempt to clarify a witness's statement ("Are you referring to Mr. Sigfrid? That tall gentleman sitting over there?") reveals his presence at the trial.[25]

If Julie Shepherd was not the mastermind, then Carl Sigfrid makes a much better candidate than Darl Shepherd. Quite possibly, Carl and Julie were the schemers and Darl was elected to do the dirty work because of his position in the outside world: Julie could hardly have been expected to seek out typhoid germs, and Sigfrid would have wanted to keep a low profile in Chicago.

FOLIE À DEUX

In Christchurch, New Zealand, in 1954, sixteen-year-old Pauline Parker and fifteen-year-old Juliet Hulme brutally murdered Parker's mother with a brick wrapped in a stocking because they believed the mother was trying to keep them apart. According to the crown prosecutor in his opening statement at their trial, the girls believed that "the mother of the accused Parker was an obstacle in their path."[26]

Parker and Hulme are classic examples of what is known as "folie à deux" (madness shared by two people), or shared psychotic disorder.[27] In folie à deux, two individuals, who by themselves would never commit a violent crime, combine to form a lethal combination that is stronger than each person in it. Well-known couples who were thought to be subject to this include Bonnie Parker and Clyde Barrow, Ian Brady and Myra Hindley, Martha Beck and Raymond Fernandez, Charlie Starkweather and Caril Ann Fugate, and Nathan Leopold and Richard Loeb. What is needed is a dominant personality to hold sway over a submissive one, and for both to share the same delusion. They may come to believe that murder or violence is necessary—and justified—for the purpose of achieving a goal that is the subject of the delusion or in counteracting a perceived attack.

One of the psychiatrists in the Leopold-Loeb case had this to say about why the two teenagers killed Bobby Franks:

> I think the Franks crime was perhaps the inevitable outcome of this curious coming together of two pathologically disordered personalities, each of whom brought into the relationship a phase of their personality which made their contemplation and the execution of this crime possible.[28]

Another commented that "[t]he psychiatric cause for this is not to be found in either boy alone, but in the interplay or interweaving of their two personalities."[29]

Typically, the delusion shared by two people in a folie à deux relationship is begun in the primary person and then duplicated in the submissive person. It is usually "persecutory or grandiose in nature," and the primary person is often susceptible to paranoid thoughts. This diagnosis fits the personality profile of Julie Shepherd, whose public statements could be termed both grandiose and paranoid ("They are all trying to keep us from our money, but I will be vindicated and borne on the shoulders of the people"); and the "lack of personal responsibility" factor of the submissive partner fits Darl Shepherd. Folie à deux partners are devoid of introspection or insight into their problems, insisting that their delusions are real happenings.[30]

In one case, a wife bought into her husband's delusion that he was being followed by prostitutes, and she eventually became convinced that these prostitutes were coming into their home with the intention of harming and humiliating her. She and her husband planned the blowing up of a building where they thought these women lived, and the husband was arrested for attempted arson. But the idea was the wife's, although he was the one trying to implement it; she also thought her husband should kidnap a policeman for ransom. In this case, the husband and wife switched roles in their folie à deux, with the husband being the dominant person in the beginning and the wife taking over that role as the disease progressed in both of them.[31]

Were Julie and Darl Shepherd subject to folie à deux, believing that everything that stood in the way of their financial security must be done away with? Were the McClintocks "obstacle[s] in their path"? Julie's paranoid rantings about a conspiracy certainly indicate mental instability. Her seeming dependence on her husband (as witnessed by Isabelle Pope) could indicate her need for a partner who bought into her vision of the world, as was clearly the case with Nathan Leopold and Richard Loeb. In that sense, she would, indeed, consider him crucial to her well-being, and this would be the source of the power he had over her.

In light of this, then, it becomes a more distinct possibility that these two poisoned Julie's brother Otto in Salina, Kansas, in 1904, as was rumored. This enabled Darl to take over the jointly held drugstore completely, but it may also have been that Otto—whose father had purchased the business to begin with and who may have felt he held some seniority rights because of this—intended to take steps to remove his brother-in-law from the partnership with a buyout or some other means. Darl Shepherd was lazy and not accustomed to working, and he was probably not pulling his weight in the business while, at the same time, sharing the profits. A threat to the Shepherds' livelihood would make Otto an obstacle that needed to be removed.

SHEPHERD'S EARLY TYPHOID RESEARCH

As early as 1917, William Darling Shepherd was thinking about typhoid and apparently had already studied it, according to his conversation with restaurant owner Louis Sbarbaro at that time. He had some connection with typhoid specialist Dr. Margaret Bodek, who was involved in a land deal with Julie Shepherd and their friend Thomas Newman in 1921. Does this mean that the plot to kill Billy McClintock was in place all along? That is not at all clear.

There may not even have been a plot to kill Emma McClintock at the start, but when matters came to a head in May 1909, her death became a necessity to the Shepherds. At that point they may have felt that if Billy didn't die, it was effort wasted in killing his mother and in making sure Julie was appointed his guardian. Shepherd's early forays into acquiring knowledge of bacterial poisoning could have been pure scientific interest on his part, or they could indicate extreme pre-planning. They could also have been done in a spirit of a fallback plan in case it was needed: Darl would bone up on bacteria to decide the best one to use if it came to that, and the Shepherds would hope that Billy's generosity would prevail when he came into his kingdom.

Still another possibility is that, as it became more and more evident that Billy was pulling away from the Shepherds—around

1922, when he was at Dartmouth and the relationship with Isabelle was getting very serious—they decided to use what was at hand: Darl's interest in bacteria, which he had studied off and on for years for no specific purpose. (If he had studied with any intensity from 1917, he would have had more knowledge of various bacteria. Judging from his inquiries in 1923 and 1924, he hadn't even decided on which germs would be most effective to use.)

If this were the case and Shepherd had great gaps in his knowledge that he needed to fill fast, he would have had to rely very heavily on what he learned from Charles Faiman. The prosecution felt that his approaching Dr. Fosberg for information after he had consulted Faiman was done as a check on what Faiman told him.[32] He would have known exactly what type of "doctor" Faiman was—it was, after all, the reason he approached him in the first place—but he wouldn't have been able to trust him completely.

SHEPHERD'S DIAGNOSIS

Why did Darl Shepherd expose himself by telling two different people—Isabelle Pope and Lewis McArthur at the Northern Trust—that Billy thought he (Billy) had typhoid? It came back to haunt him when he was suspected of poisoning his ward and reflected, or so the prosecution claimed, his guilty conscience.[33] The damning thing here is that he made the statements before an official diagnosis had been made, yet he had said nothing to anyone who could have acted on this early knowledge.

Here we see another example of Darl Shepherd's tendency to be a blabbermouth, something that should have given pause to whichever person in his life was running the show (Julie or Sigfrid, or possibly both). He had obviously not thought this out clearly before making the statements. In fact, Isabelle had asked him why he hadn't told anyone, and his response was, "Well, the treatment is the same as for the flu [which is what Billy was being treated for], so they haven't lost anything."[34] This was another mistake, in that the treatments were NOT the same, and someone who had studied typhoid, as Shepherd had claimed to, should have known this. It still doesn't explain his failure to present the possibility that they were dealing with typhoid and not flu.

Perhaps Shepherd thought that if it were believed that the victim himself thought he had typhoid and was not surprised by it (because of having eaten oysters), then no one would bother to investigate further.

THE TIMING OF BILLY'S ILLNESS

Billy's ingestion of oysters at the Windermere House restaurant on November 3 was exactly on pace for the onset of his typhoid fever on November 21: an eighteen-day incubation period. Doesn't this seem to indicate that perhaps his typhoid did, after all, come from those oysters? Not necessarily.

First of all, it must be remembered that there were four people in Billy's party that evening, and three of them ordered oysters. Only Billy got typhoid. No other Windermere patron got typhoid from the hotel's shellfish until three weeks after Billy died.

Billy loved oysters, and everyone knew it. He ordered them frequently when he dined out, and Darl Shepherd admitted buying them on occasion and bringing them home for his ward to enjoy.[35] The Shepherds may have been waiting for their chance to feed Billy the germs, and once he told them he had eaten oysters, the eighteen-day window opened up for them. Now they could begin infecting his water.

CONCLUSION

Out of the endless permutations and possibilities of this case—was it possible to kill someone with typhoid germs? whose idea was it? when was it initiated? how long had it been planned?—there is only one thing that is clear: Billy McClintock was murdered. To support a finding of natural death, it is necessary to find all the following elements to be merely coincidental occurrences:

1. *The death of Emma McClintock.* She died of mercury poisoning after visiting the Shepherds in Bay View, leaving Julie Shepherd in charge of her son. An autopsy in 1925 determined the death to be intentional homicide.

2. *Billy's will.* Instead of leaving his money to his fiancee, or waiting until his marriage to make a will at all, Billy signed an instrument on his twenty-first birthday, the very day he was entitled to inherit his parents' estate, leaving all to William Darling Shepherd.

3. *Billy's death.* Billy happened to die within the very short span of time that would allow William Darling Shepherd to inherit the fortune

under the will: between April 3, 1924, and February 22, 1925. When he died there were only two and a half months left until his wedding, which would have voided the April 3 will.

How likely is it that all three of these events—particularly an intentional homicide that opened the door to wealth for the Shepherds—were coincidences? It may not be certain *how* they did it, but it is certain *that* they did it.

We can never know for sure the answers to all the questions raised by this case. Whether the idea originated with Julie Shepherd or Carl Sigfrid—or both—will remain a mystery. What is not a mystery, however, is the murder of Emma McClintock, and that one fact indicates that her son was murdered, too. Otherwise, what was the point?

Whatever Billy's feelings for his guardians as he grew older, he would have provided for them out of a sense of gratitude. But they were not satisfied with a house and a pension. They wanted it all. Would they prevail in the will contest that followed the trial and achieve the Fatal Fortune at last?

Chapter 8

The Will Contest

*This young man was raised to manhood that he might make a will
and then be killed.*

—Judge Harry Olson

Before Darl and Julie could get their hands on the Fatal Fortune,
they would have to emerge victorious from the will contest now
filed by nine of Billy's cousins (all related to his father). The
grounds would be undue influence because of Shepherd's fiduciary relationship to Billy; invalidity because not all the witnesses
were in the presence of each other when it was signed; and
invalidity because the witnesses were servants in the employ of
Shepherd.[1] In the event the cousins were unsuccessful, Isabelle
Pope was waiting in the wings to file her own suit for a widow's
share. Her agreement with the cousins was that, whichever party
was successful—Isabelle or the heirs—they would split the estate
in half.

The cousins were all in the Eaton family, relatives of William
McClintock Sr. through his sister—including his niece Maude
Eaton Walker, who had come to visit Emma after her uncle's
death. Billy had met only two of these cousins in his lifetime,
and it was asserted that he strongly disliked one of those two.[2]
It was the old story of relatives coming out of the woodwork

after the death of someone they barely knew and insisting they were owed some or all of the estate. In this case, however, it would serve the purpose of keeping the money from the grasping hands of the Shepherds, at least for a time and maybe permanently.

There was enough shadiness surrounding the will to cause the cousins, miffed at having been left out of a share of McClintock Sr.'s estate, to come forward and try to break it. They may even have been notified by Judge Olson after Billy's death, as their interference would suit his purposes in thwarting the Shepherds: even if the Shepherds got away with murder, they wouldn't be able to spend the money.

Immediately after Shepherd's acquittal, the cousins filed their suit. The contest would take four years and fill up five boxes in the probate court archives. The funds were frozen for that time, leaving the Shepherds unable to tap the estate.

But what, exactly, were they all fighting over?

When William McClintock Sr. died, his estate consisted of money; stocks; promissory notes for money loaned; and real estate holdings in Chicago, Iowa, Texas, South Dakota, and Saskatchewan, Canada (some of these had been purchased by his first wife, Sarah Hickling). He also had 10,400 shares in the Arizona-based Braganza Gold Mining Company, valued at $100 per share.[3] (Was Darl Shepherd checking out the mine on his visit to Arizona at the time Dr. Fosberg said Shepherd was consulting with him about typhoid in Chicago? If so, it could indicate premeditation in that, under normal circumstances, Shepherd would not be getting those mine shares at all. They were Billy's.)

McClintock Sr. held mortgages on some of the property, and the downtown Chicago parcels consisted of office and apartment buildings. He was like a one-man bank and kept a monthly schedule of what money was due from whom on what day: for notes, for mortgages, or for rent. When debtors didn't pay, he sued, and he had at least one mortgage foreclosure in the works. At the time of his death in 1907, there was a criminal case pending against him, possibly for criminal negligence at not having a fire escape in one of his buildings where a fire had occurred.

When Emma McClintock died in June 1909, her husband's estate had barely been settled. She was in the process of collecting her dower rights, selling off most of the properties, and deciding what to do with the rest. This was what Alexander Reichmann was taking care of, and a look at the itemization papers he filed to support his fee claim gives the impression that he and his partners devoted practically every working day from May 1907 (McClintock's death) to June 1909 (Emma's death) to the McClintock estate. It was a busy portfolio with many actions pending.

Aside from his own law practice with the firm of Judah, Willard, Wolf & Reichmann, Alexander Reichmann was associated with the Northern Trust. When Emma was dying he suggested that she place her estate in trust for Billy with that organization. Reichmann knew that if no trust were in place, the Shepherds would plunder it before Billy came of age. When Emma's estate was finally settled, Billy's trust—after expenses were paid—was worth about $600,000, considerably less than it was when McClintock Sr. died.[4]

Emma had left generous cash bequests to quite a few people, mostly her own cousins, but also to Julie Shepherd ($5,000); her maid Stella Costigan ($2,000); her church, the Second Presbyterian Church of Chicago ($5,000); and Bethany College in Kansas ($5,000).[5] Other than Julie Shepherd, who would be taking care of her son, and the charities, the only non-relative receiving a bequest was Stella Costigan. Emma McClintock must have felt a kinship with the young woman, whose husband John had died when they were both in their twenties, leaving her to raise their little girl alone.[6]

When Billy turned twenty-one and the estate was turned over to him (which now included both his mother's share and what he had previously inherited from his father), he elected to leave much of it with the Northern Trust for safekeeping and as an investment. This was why Darl Shepherd had to go to the trust for house money when Billy was sick and couldn't sign a check. (They didn't give it to Darl, though, until one of the officers went to the Kenilworth house and got Billy's okay first.)[7] The young man would have received a whopping $51,000 in income annually,[8] equivalent to over half a million dollars today.

According to Darl Shepherd, he and Billy had a discussion about his will and its provisions during Billy's Christmas break from Dartmouth in 1923. Shepherd told him he couldn't draw up the will because of his fiduciary relationship and also because he was a beneficiary. Billy supposedly said that it didn't matter because he preferred to keep his business private rather than go to an attorney he didn't know. Darl suggested the $8,000 annuity to Isabelle Pope to protect her before the wedding. Billy was worried, Shepherd claimed, that if he died before the wedding, "another fellow" would be spending his money if he were to leave it all to Isabelle now.[9]

At some point in the next few months, Billy supposedly wrote to Darl and included a memorandum of terms he wanted included in the will. He would then sign it when he went home for spring break, which coincided with his twenty-first birthday. Shepherd told his secretary, young Eva Peterson, "The kid wants me to write his will," and they drafted it in his office. Eva never actually saw the memorandum, nor did anyone else. Shepherd kept saying he would produce it if necessary, but it was never forthcoming. As to the letter Billy sent with it, Shepherd said, "I don't keep personal letters."[10]

Here are the provisions of Billy's will, after the usual statement regarding paying off debts:[11]

> Second. I give and bequeath to my affianced wife, ISABELLE POPE, the sum of EIGHT THOUSAND DOLLARS ($8,000.00) per annum for the term of her life. I make this bequest as a token of the love and affection I have for her, and as a proper protection for her until such time as our marriage shall be consummated. **The arranging for, and the manner of making the payments of this bequest I leave to the discretion of my Executor hereinafter named.** (emphasis added)

> Third. I give, devise, and bequeath to my foster father, WILLIAM D. SHEPHERD, all the rest and residue of my property of whatsoever description, both real and personal of which I may die possessed or to which I may be entitled. I make this bequest for the benefit of my foster parents as a token of my love and affection for them and as a mark of appreciation of the years of care that they have given me during which time they have in all manners [sic] been all that parents could be to me. I do not make a special bequest to my beloved foster mother JULIE M. SHEPHERD, knowing full well that through this bequest she will obtain all the benefits thereof without the worry and care incident to possession of the property itself.

> Fourth. I name and appoint my foster father WILLIAM D. SHEPHERD to be the Executor of this my last Will and Testament, imposing on him the sacred duty of carrying out my wishes and desires in the bequest above mentioned.

How did Shepherd get Billy to make the annuity to Isabelle so flexible? Probably by telling him that if she got married, he,

Shepherd, would cut it off so the "other fellow" wouldn't be spending Billy's money.

At the trial Robert Crowe had tried to get in some questions regarding the language used in the third provision, that it was Darl's and not Billy's, but he was not allowed to.

The will was signed on April 3, 1924, Billy's twenty-first birthday. The witnesses were two servants in the McClintock-Shepherd home: Marie Gartner, a maid; and Eva Nelson, the "cranky" cook (no relation to Emma). Wills are supposed to be signed with the maker and the witnesses together in the same room, with the maker stating that this is his will and the witnesses signing in the presence of each other. Yet Eva Nelson had said at one time that she was down in the basement doing laundry when William Shepherd had her sign the will, and that nobody else was there. Shepherd gave both her and Marie Gartner $5 for signing. Eva later retracted this statement, claiming that it was "Mr. Billy" who had asked her and that it was done in the drawing room with everyone else there.[12]

Marie Gartner stated that she had been working in the kitchen when Billy asked her to come to the drawing room and that everything had been done properly. She added, however, that at the inquest, Assistant State's Attorney John Sbarbaro had threatened to have her deported back to Sweden if she didn't say that she signed the will somewhere other than the drawing room.[13] (Possibly Sbarbaro thought she was lying and was trying to get her to tell the truth, but this threat of deportation could also explain why Eva Nelson—also from Sweden—might have changed her story.)

During the first will hearing in November, while Shepherd was waiting outside the courtroom, he was physically attacked by little Louis Kles, the former chauffeur. "You killed Billy, you dirty dog!" Kles shouted as he struck the much larger Shepherd twice on the chin. A deputy sheriff intervened and hauled him before the judge who was hearing the will testimony. Kles was fined $50 for contempt of court. The irate chauffeur also claimed that Shepherd still owed him $55 in wages but refused to pay it.[14]

Kles said he was at the courthouse because he thought he was to be a witness at the will contest. At the inquest, he maintained that Eva Nelson and Marie Gartner had been coached to say that Billy, and not William Darling Shepherd, asked them to sign the will.[15] The implication is that Billy might not have made out the will after all.

Probate Judge Henry Horner did an odd thing after the hearings concluded. At first he indicated that he would be inclined to admit the will to probate, at which time Orville Taylor—the lawyer representing the cousins—seemed resigned to allow that to happen so he could appeal the decision in circuit court. Everybody expected the next words to be the judge's sustaining of the will as valid, but he paused instead and told Taylor that he would be willing to hear arguments and evidence of undue influence on the following day. It was as if Horner were trying to communicate a hint to Taylor that he might deny the will if Taylor could come up with something stronger than he already had.

At that point, a former senator representing an unnamed client stood up and, in spite of his apparent lack of standing in the case, was allowed to argue that since Shepherd, the beneficiary, drew up the will, it constituted a *prima facie* case of undue influence. The fact that Shepherd's own servants, over whom he had dominion, were the witnesses was another proof of it. Once the witnesses were disqualified, there would be no will, the ex-senator argued.

Sure enough, at the next hearing, Judge Horner *denied* the admission of the will to probate based on a presumption of undue influence. Not that there actually *was* undue influence, he clarified, but the presumption was there and it was his duty under the laws of Illinois to deny probate. It was up to the Shepherds to overcome the presumption, and this they had not done. (They had been served with a subpoena to produce the famous memorandum, and this decision seems to indicate that they did not do so, although whether they did or not was never stated.) Shepherd's attorney promptly filed an appeal with the circuit court.[16]

But here was Shepherd's dilemma: If he lost on appeal to the circuit court, he could continue to appeal all the way up to the Supreme Court, if that august body wished to hear the matter. If he kept losing, he would be forced to appeal if he wanted any of the McClintock assets. However, even if he won at any point along the way, the eight heirs would then begin their own appeals process following that same route. Should the heirs ultimately lose, Isabelle Pope would then file her own suit as "equitable widow." Years and years of litigation faced all the parties at this point.

Shepherd did win on appeal, after two years, but the circuit judge—even as he overturned the lower court's decision—pointed out ways in which the McClintock will could be broken, so it was not much of a victory.[17] The cousins then began their own quest for the Fatal Fortune through the courts. In September 1927, Isabelle Pope—possibly tiring of the prolonged delays or possibly desirous of forcing a settlement—filed her own widow's portion suit, even while the cousins' suit was still pending.[18]

In the meantime, estate taxes and lawyers' fees were devouring the estate's assets, so in 1929 the parties finally agreed to an out-of-court settlement whereby Shepherd would get half and Isabelle and the heirs (now ten in number) would split the remaining half.[19] How much was the estate worth by then? The highest figure had it at $500,000, so the most the Shepherds could have received would be $250,000, and that figure may be overly generous. Isabelle Pope probably got about $125,000, although one report said she got $300,000—which was unlikely, as it was higher than the half to be shared by her and the cousins.[20]

What of the dream team, William Scott Stewart and William W. O'Brien? Originally, they had stated they would be Shepherd's lawyers for the will contest—no doubt to protect their financial interests—but when the proceedings began a month after the trial ended, Shepherd was represented by his old friend and former partner, Robert Stoll. Stewart and O'Brien probably opted out when they saw what a long, uphill battle it would be and with no guarantee of success.

In the end, then, Billy McClintock got a measure of justice in that Isabelle Pope was awarded some of his estate and the Shepherds had to wait four years before they could get their hands on a greatly devalued share.

How did the Fatal Fortune fare in the hands of the Shepherds? Did the curse wreak its vengeance on them?

Chapter 9

Epilogue

I had my husband just the same and my children and my house like any other woman. A good house too and a good husband that I loved and fine children out of him.
—Katherine Anne Porter, "The Jilting of Granny Weatherall"

For the most part, the colorful cast of characters involved in the Shepherd-McClintock drama did not disappoint in their after-trial lives. Some strove for anonymity, with varying degrees of success, while others sought the spotlight. Still others lived drab existences compared to their sensational parts in this saga, their one moment in the spotlight the high (or low) point of their lives.

THE REPORTERS

Maureen McKernan, who interviewed Isabelle Pope on the train and also covered the trial for the *Chicago Tribune*, had previously worked for the *Chicago Herald and Examiner*. Immediately after the Leopold and Loeb sentence hearing concluded in September 1924, McKernan—with the blessing of the defense—published *The Amazing Crime and Trial of Leopold and Loeb*. Clarence Darrow and one of the other defense attorneys wrote prefaces to it.[1]

McKernan's book was mostly a compilation of documents in the case, including the entire text of Darrow's twelve-hour summation pleading for the life of the two boys. However, she omitted several sections of the psychiatric report, which detailed homosexual behavior, and also changed some of the salty language used by the two defendants in their confessions.

McKernan eventually moved to New York City, where she worked for the *New York Post*. In 1938 she scored a coup by getting two lengthy interviews with the widow of slain mobster Dutch Schultz.[2]

Genevieve Forbes Herrick, in partnership with her husband John, wrote *The Life of William Jennings Bryan* in 1925.[3] In 1928 she covered the Republican convention for WGN radio. (WGN, which stands for "World's Greatest Newspaper," was, and still is, owned by the *Chicago Tribune*, Herrick's employer.)[4] When Al Capone was let out of prison in 1929 after serving time for tax evasion, he agreed to an interview with Mrs. Herrick, the only one he granted.[5] In 1942 Herrick was chosen by Mrs. Oveta Culp Hobby to be the public relations advisor for the newly formed Women's Auxiliary Army Corps (WAAC).[6]

Genevieve Herrick was greatly admired by Eleanor Roosevelt, who encouraged women journalists by holding frequent press conferences with them at the White House.[7] Mrs. Herrick, like Maureen McKernan, also left the Midwest and wrote for various publications in the East, notably *Country Gentleman* magazine.[8] She died in 1962, the same year as Eleanor Roosevelt.[9]

THE LAWYERS

Judge Thomas Lynch was still on the bench when he died in July 1950 at age seventy.[10]

A month after the Shepherd trial, the two defense attorneys—William Scott Stewart and William W. O'Brien—succeeded in getting a death row inmate's sentence commuted to life by claiming that his three close encounters with the hangman had caused him to lose his mind.[11]

That September, O'Brien's wife divorced him, charging "drunkenness and cruelty," and asked for $850 a month in alimony.[12]

In October 1926, O'Brien was defending notorious gang leader Joe Saltis for the murder of a rival and had just finished selecting a jury for that trial. He got into an automobile with Earl "Hymie" Weiss, the late Dion O'Banion's successor; Paddy Murray and Sam Peller, other O'Banion gang members; and Benny Jacobs, O'Brien's investigator. The group got out at O'Banion's former florist shop (and the site of his murder), now run by his partner, and immediately they were fired upon by machine guns from an upper-story window across the street and from a car driving by.

Weiss and Murray were killed immediately and the other three wounded. O'Brien was hit in the stomach and also in the chest, but the latter shots were prevented from hitting his heart by the inches-thick papers he had in his breast pocket. (The same thing had once saved Theodore Roosevelt from assassination.)[13]

O'Brien, still conscious, vowed that the defense of Saltis would continue and that they would win. As he was about to undergo surgery, he declared, "I want my associate [Frank McDonnell] to go ahead with the defense of Saltis on Wednesday. We can win that case and I want McDonnell to go ahead with it whether I die or not."

As he had in 1921 when he was shot in the saloon, O'Brien refused to name his assailants. But police already knew who they were: Al Capone's gang.

Upstairs in the florist shop, in the safe of O'Banion's partner, police found a list of witnesses who would be testifying for the prosecution in the Saltis case. Was the plan to bribe or intimidate them? Was O'Brien at the florist shop to get this list? On the same piece of paper were the names of all the prospective jurors in the case, and rumors were rampant that the Saltis jury had been "fixed."

O'Brien tried to distance himself from the O'Banion gang by claiming that he had not been in the Hymie Weiss automobile, but just happened to be in the neighborhood after getting off a street-car. But the timing and the evidence did not support this claim.

O'Brien survived his wounds, consulting by telephone with his partner about the trial, and Joe Saltis won his case. After the acquittal, O'Brien filed a slander suit on behalf of Saltis against John Stege, Chicago's captain of detectives, for $100,000. According-ing to the suit, Stege had said some not-so-nice things about Saltis in the newspapers, and thus had "injured his good name, credit, and reputation, and had brought him into public scandal and disgrace."[14]

In 1932 W. W. O'Brien formed a third political party and ran an unsuccessful race for governor on that ticket.[15] In 1935 he defended an accomplice of the notorious Baby Face Nelson and, although there was no acquittal this time, the defendant got a life sentence instead of death.[16]

O'Brien's former partner, William Scott Stewart, also continued his involvement with the mob. In 1931 he was among a group of several lawyers involved in a payroll padding case on the part of the Sanitary District, and it was recommended that he receive a one-year suspension.[17]

In 1933 Stewart represented one of Chicago's most infamous gangsters, Roger "The Terrible" Touhy, on a charge of kidnapping. Although he really was the victim of a frame-up engineered by a rival mob and not guilty of the kidnapping, Touhy was convicted. He escaped from Joliet Prison, was captured, escaped again and was recaptured. He eventually got out of prison in 1959, only to be gunned down a month later.[18]

In 1941 Stewart published an article in *Esquire* magazine entitled "How to Beat the Lie Detector," supposedly the first ever written on this topic.[19]

When the Kefauver Committee on Organized Crime was formed in 1950, one of those subpoenaed to appear was a former Capone gangster named Paul "The Waiter" Ricca. Stewart, who was Ricca's attorney, refused to accept the subpoena.[20]

State's Attorney Robert E. Crowe died at age seventy-eight on January 19, 1958, just two months before the man who made him nationally famous, Nathan Leopold, was freed on parole. (Richard Loeb had died in prison a few years after they were sent to Joliet, the result of a knife attack by another inmate.)[21]

Alexander F. Reichmann, attorney for the McClintocks and the nemesis of the Shepherds, achieved the Holy Grail of the legal profession: in 1942 he argued a case before the U.S. Supreme Court, representing the respondent in *Harrison v. Northern Trust*.[22] Prior to that, he was responsible for getting over $8 million for the widow of J. Ogden Armour (of Armour & Company, the meatpackers) with the sale of some oil stocks previously thought worthless. For his share, Reichmann got $1,402,794, which in 1931 was worth nearly $17 million in today's money. He died in Kenilworth in the 1950s.[23]

Dr. AMANTE RONGETTI

Rongetti, who had fabricated a meeting with William Darling Shepherd and was exposed on the stand during cross-examination, was a legitimate doctor with a legitimate hospital (called, variously, Ashland Boulevard Hospital, Rongetti Hospital, and West End Hospital). But he fell afoul of the law with his abortion services. In fact, his testifying for the prosecution in the Shepherd case may have been prompted by the hope that he would fare better with his legal problems.

In 1928 Rongetti was convicted of murdering nineteen-year-old Loretta Enders on his operating table. He was the first man sentenced to die in Illinois's electric chair and the first surgeon to have the death penalty imposed because a patient died during an abortion. The reason for the harsh sentence was that Rongetti had refused to attend to Enders's health complications because she had not paid her bill. His attorney in this matter was William Scott Stewart, who obviously did not hold it against Rongetti that he had testified against Shepherd in 1925.[24]

In 1929 the Illinois Supreme Court reversed this verdict because of an error in the jury instructions. Rongetti was found guilty of manslaughter and sent to Joliet Prison, but this, too, was reversed and he was pardoned.[25]

In 1929 Rongetti was brought to trial for the murder of Elizabeth Palumbo, who also died of complications from an illegal abortion. However, he was found not guilty in that case.[26]

THE SUNSHINE GIRL

Estelle Gehling, William Shepherd's mistress, married Frank Daniel and later divorced him. She died in Dunbar, Wisconsin, the resident city of her parents, in January 1972.[27]

THE SERVANTS

Stella Costigan and her daughter Maud, who was three years older than Billy, stayed on for a while after Emma died. Then Stella met and married a farmer named Harry Carson, and they moved to Linden, Iowa, with Maud.[28]

Anna Anderson was dismissed right after Emma died. She married a man named Beckford and moved to the suburb of Oak Park, Illinois.[29]

Louis Kles does not appear in any databases after 1925.[30]

HARRY OLSON

Harry Olson's brilliant career as a lawyer and a jurist has been unfortunately overshadowed by his outspoken philosophy of the causes of crime. Olson believed that criminals were mentally retarded or mentally ill and that the weakness could be traced to genetics. He thought such people should be sterilized so they could not reproduce and became a spokesman for the eugenics movement. He advocated strict immigration laws, whereby only the mentally sound would be allowed into the United States.[31]

Ironically, Harry's own son, Harry Jr., was severely mentally handicapped as the result of an accident during birth that deprived the infant of oxygen to the brain. However, by Olson's own definition, the boy would not have been subject to sterilization, as his retardation was not the result of genetics.

Shortly before his death in 1935, Harry Olson wrote proudly of his work being the model of eugenics laws in Germany, where Adolf Hitler was at that time in power:

> [Harry Laughlin and I] collaborated in drafting the eugenical sterilization law passed by the Virginia Legislature and sustained by the United States Supreme Court, after which 32 states have passed the law and also Germany recently.

It is almost certain that Olson did not know what was going on in Germany at that time, and in his own life he was a kind and compassionate man. While other eugenicists took aim at certain races, Olson did not, but felt that the theories should be applied to all who fit the profile of the criminally defective. Still, the discovery casts a shadow over the judicial work of Judge Olson. He is included, albeit in a minor way, in Edwin Black's 2003 work *War against the Weak: Eugenics and America's Campaign to Create a Master Race.*

REVEREND CARL NAUMANN

Rev. Naumann disappeared from the limelight, continuing his pastorate at St. Paul's Lutheran Church in Evanston and presumably his friendship with the Shepherds. He died in July 1942 at age sixty-eight.[32]

CHARLES FAIMAN

When we last saw Charles Faiman, he was running out of the Cook County courthouse, the charges against him dismissed for the moment. He and his wife Louise ended up in Florida, where their son was born, and by 1930 they had settled in Euless, Texas, near Fort Worth. He continued to list himself as a physician.[33]

Faiman continued his errant ways and was arrested in Texas for prescribing an abortifacient for a woman when he was not a licensed physician.[34]

Charles Faiman died of a heart attack in a nursing home at age seventy-six, on July 9, 1976. (Ironically, his residence was located on South Sheppard Drive.) On his death certificate, Faiman is listed as a physician.[35]

CARL J. SIGFRID

Sigfrid continued to live with Erin Gilbert as common-law husband and wife until she left him some time after 1930. She continued to call herself Erin Sigfrid, eventually dying in California under that name in 1962 at age eighty-two.[36] In 1931, Sigfrid's ex-wife Elice died, and in 1942 he married Clare Rhea.[37]

Sigfrid moved to Denver in 1935 to be the attorney for the Denver & Rio Grande Railroad, but continued to represent clients in Ouray for a while after that. He retired in 1956 and died in Denver two years later at age eighty-six, having established himself as "the most knowledgeable and skillful specialist in mining law of all attorneys in Colorado."[38]

ISABELLE POPE

Isabelle went back to teaching after the trial.[39] The will contest was settled in 1929, and on September 28 of that year she married a man who had been at New Trier High School with her and Billy, and who was a friend of both: Melvin Veeder, himself an heir to a fortune made by his maternal grandfather, M. J. Neahr, who had founded a bag company. Veeder, who was ahead of Billy and Isabelle in high school, had gone to Yale and made a mark for himself as a champion swimmer. At the time of their marriage he was working as an executive at a printing company.[40]

After a honeymoon in Europe, Isabelle and Melvin settled in Winnetka, where they raised three daughters and a son. Isabelle did not tell her children about Billy McClintock until 1950, when the *Chicago Tribune* did a front-page "where are they now?" retrospective on the twenty-fifth anniversary of the case.

Knowing that her oldest daughter would probably encounter some comments and questions at school, Isabelle sat her down and said, "I have to tell you something."[41]

But Isabelle kept this part of her life very private and did not talk about it with her children until after their father died. Then, the murder of a family acquaintance brought it all back to her and she became very emotional. She had kept Billy's letters, some photos, and all of the clippings from the newspapers, and before she died she made her children promise they would not throw them out. Isabelle's daughters could see that, even decades after Billy's death, it affected their mother tremendously and there were aspects of it that she still found difficult to talk about.[42]

After Melvin died in 1964, Isabelle married Randy Harrington and outlived him as well. Isabelle Pope Veeder Harrington died in California, where the family had eventually settled, in 1997 at age ninety-four.[43]

THE SHEPHERDS

William Darling Shepherd and Julia Graf Shepherd slipped back into oblivion after the will contest. Despite evading criminal sanctions for the death of Billy McClintock and despite inheriting his estate after all, it must have taken its toll on them. They would have had to come up with some payment for the dream team, Stewart and O'Brien, and the estate was severely depleted by the time it was settled in 1929.

Nor do they seem to have been living the high life. By 1930 the Shepherds had sold the large Kenilworth home and moved to a smaller place right around the corner, but with no live-in servants as they had been accustomed to since 1907.[44] Eventually, they moved to Glenview, about seven miles west of Kenilworth and away from the Gold Coast towns. In 1941 Darl Shepherd developed chronic myocarditis and prostate problems. A year later, on May 30, 1942, he was rushed to St. Francis Hospital in Evanston, where he died of uremia at age sixty-seven. There is no reference to diabetes on his death certificate, which is normally included as a contributing factor, despite the Shepherds' trying to play that card back in 1925 when Darl was in jail. Shepherd is buried in Des Plaines, another northern Chicago suburb.[45]

Shepherd made out a will in 1932 after the McClintock estate problems were finally settled, witnessed by his former partner Robert H. Stoll and his stenographer Eva M. Peterson. Everything went to his wife, Julie. In the paragraph bequeathing his property to her, he added this line: "This will in no wise repay her for the love and loyalty she has shown me, but is the best that I can do."[46] Although many might have thought it referred to his legal troubles in 1925, it more than likely refers to the Sunshine Girl episode and any others like it. There is an undercurrent of guilt to it.

Darl Shepherd's mother and stepfather had died by 1942, but all of his siblings (except Alice, who had died before 1900) were still alive: Gussie, who was younger than Darl, and Preston and Henry, who were older.

After Darl died, Julie moved in with her nephew, John A. Graf, an attorney who lived in Evanston (her siblings had followed the Shepherds from Kansas to Chicago by 1920). He represented Darl's estate and filed the required executrix documents for her.[47]

One of Darl Shepherd's statements seems to have come true: he had told a reporter in 1925 that he would break up the estate into smaller portions to defeat the Fatal Fortune's curse. He broke it up, all right—by going through it. Eighteen years after Billy McClintock's death, all that was left to pass on to Julie Shepherd were three parcels of real estate, 340 shares of stock, and $567.44 in cash.

The real estate all came from William McClintock Sr.'s estate: the 581 acres in Chambers County, Texas, which was the Bay View parcel with the cottage on it, where Emma McClintock had been poisoned; and two properties in Saskatchewan, which had come from McClintock's first wife, Sarah Hickling. The stock certificates, except for sixty shares in the Major Engineering Corporation, were in the Indiana Limestone Corporation, all purchased in 1931 and 1933. Gone were the Braganza Gold Mining shares and the other stocks that Emma McClintock had passed to Billy.

Although Julie Shepherd was sixty-four at Darl's death, at some point after that she married a man named William Gough, who also predeceased her. She died in a nursing home in Evanston on April 13, 1970, of long-standing heart disease just before her ninety-third birthday, and is buried next to Darl Shepherd in Ridgewood Cemetery.[48] By the time Julie Shepherd Gough died, the real estate parcels and stock shares had been sold, and all that was left of the Fatal Fortune was a mere $30,000.

Notes

Articles from the *Chicago Daily Tribune* and the *New York Times* have been abbreviated to *CDT* and *NYT*, respectively. All other newspaper titles will be spelled out in their entirety.

CHAPTER 1: THE FATAL FORTUNE

1. Unless otherwise indicated, the information in this chapter comes from the interviews with, and testimony of, Isabelle Pope, contained in Genevieve Forbes Herrick, "Isabelle Pope Tells Romance of McClintock," *CDT*, 24 December 1924; Genevieve Forbes Herrick, "Fiancée Tells Story," *CDT*, 25 December 1924; James Doherty, "Describes Her Betrothal and Billy's Death," *CDT*, 16 June 1925; James Doherty, "Germ 'Doctor' Appears Today; Case Nears End," *CDT*, 17 June 1925; "Youth's View of Shepherds Told in Note," *CDT*, 17 June 1925. See *NYT* for these dates as well.

2. "Shepherd Gives His M'Clintock Story to State," *CDT*, 28 December 1924.

3. "Clew Fails as Woman Looks at W. D. Shepherd," *CDT*, 6 March 1925.

4. "Crowe Outlines State's Case," *CDT*, 12 June 1925.

5. Kate N. Grossman and Rosalind Rossi, "At the Head of the Class," *Chicago Sun-Times*, 16 March 2003.

6. *New Trier Echoes* for 1921. Courtesy of New Trier High School Library.

7. Ibid.

8. Family of Isabelle Pope.

9. Phi Delta Theta's Web site at www.phideltatheta.org. Alpha Phi's Web site at www.alphaphi.org.

10. "Youth's View of Shepherds Told in Note," *CDT*, 17 June 1925.

11. Information on the popular culture of the 1920s comes from Time-Life's *Our American Century Series* (1999); *The Jazz Age*, particularly the chapter titled "Flaming Youth"; and from Lois Gordon and Alan Gordon, *American Chronicle: Six Decades in American Life, 1920–1980* (New York: Atheneum, 1987).

12. Isabelle Pope's family said that she was a lifelong Cubs fan.

13. Billy's transcript from Dartmouth College. Courtesy of Dartmouth College Library.

14. "Youth's View of Shepherds Told in Note," *CDT*, 17 June 1925.

15. "Closed Colleges," www.closedcollege.bizland.com. "Saul Bellow," www.kirjasto.sci.fi/bellow.htm.

16. Northwestern University's registrar's office.

17. "Youth's View of Shepherds Told in Note," *CDT*, 17 June 1925; "More Love Letters from Isabelle Pope to McClintock Show Her Betrothal Code," *CDT*, 18 June 1925.

18. Family of Isabelle Pope.

19. "Dartmouth Game by Game Results," at http://cfbdatawarehouse.com.

20. "I Never Saw Typhoid Germ," *CDT*, 27 December 1924. This information comes from William Shepherd and is most likely correct. Billy's grades from Dartmouth bear this out, and Shepherd would not lie about something that could be verified by talking to Billy's friends.

21. "McClintock Heir Returning," *CDT*, 26 December 1924.

22. "Typhoid Fever," at www.mayoclinic.com. Accessed 15 June 2004.

23. Tim Brown, Property Manager, Windermere House. Personal communication, 12 and 14 December 2001. See also "Windermere House" at www.metroplexinc.com/winderme.htm.

24. James Doherty, "Germ Defense Coup Fails," *CDT*, 13 June 1925.

25. "Germs Stolen, Shepherd Case Doctor Asserts," *CDT*, 1 March 1925 (McArthur); James Doherty, "Demands Faiman Be Court Witness," *CDT*, 18 June 1925.

26. "Shepherd Gives His M'Clintock Story to State," *CDT*, 28 December 1924; "Shepherd, in Chicago, Charges Enemy Plot; Threatens Reprisal," *NYT*, 28 December 1924.

27. "Shepherd, in Chicago, Charges Enemy Plot; Threatens Reprisal," *NYT*, 28 December 1924: "One reason that made us peeved at her was that she would read the nurse's chart to Billy when she came to visit him. She would even read his temperature record. The nurse finally had to hide her chart when Miss Pope came."

28. "Germ Defense Coup Fails," *CDT*, 13 June 1925.

29. "Trace Typhoid Germ Sale for McClintock Quiz," *CDT*, 25 February 1925; certificate of death of William Nelson McClintock from Cook County Vital Statistics.

30. "William McClintock's Last Testament," *CDT*, 24 December 1924.

31. "Shepherd Gives His M'Clintock Story to State," *CDT*, 28 December 1924.

32. Testimony of Louis Kles in "Says Shepherd Boasted about Future Riches," *CDT*, 26 February 1925: "He was laughing about Miss Pope, how they fooled her and all that."

33. "Intended Ushers for M'Clintock Are Pallbearers," *CDT*, 6 December 1924; "Fiancee Breaks Down at Grave of M'Clintock," *CDT*, 7 December 1924.

34. See "Find A Grave" at www.findagrave.com.

35. For information on the Fatal Fortune, see "M'Clintock Fortune Trail Darkened by Death's Shadow," *CDT*, 24 December 1924 and "Iowa Clan Unrelated," *CDT*, 26 December 1924. The story told by the nurse about Mrs. Hickling poisoning her husband is in "Shepherd Rebuffed Again on Bail Plea," *NYT*, 11 April 1925. The story about William McClintock Sr.'s possible poisoning of his first wife and the settlement with her half-brother is in "Shepherd Gets New Rebuff in Move for Bail," *CDT*, 1 April 1925.

36. "Shepherd Rebuffed Again on Bail Plea," *NYT*, 11 April 1925.

37. "Autoist Dies; Wife Saved," *CDT*, 18 May 1907; Coroner's inquest on death of William McClintock, from Illinois Regional Archives Depository, conducted 18 May 1907; certificate of death for William McClintock from Cook County Vital Records.

38. "Autoist Dies; Wife Saved," *CDT*, 18 May 1907. This article estimates the amount as $7 million, which is probably too high, but would depend on the real estate valuation.

39. Last will and testament of Emma Catherine McClintock, from Cook County Clerk's Archives.

40. "Millionaire Orphan Dead; About to Wed," *CDT*, 5 December 1924. The article calls Sigfrid the brother of Mrs. Shepherd, and William Shepherd is almost certainly the source of this, as he is being interviewed. However, he was her first cousin: in the 1880 census he is living with Mrs. Shepherd's family, the Grafs, and is listed as the nephew of the head of the household.

41. "'Killed for Greed'—Crowe," *CDT*, 12 June 1925.

42. "'Indict Defamers'—Shepherd," *CDT*, 29 December 1924.

43. "'Killed for Greed'—Crowe," *CDT*, 12 June 1925.

44. "Crowe Piles Up Evidence for Shepherd Trial," *CDT*, 2 May 1925.

45. "Says Shepherd Boasted about Future Riches," *CDT*, 26 February 1925.

46. "Mrs. Shepherd Held to Jail," *CDT*, 6 May 1925. Olson also said he had gotten a letter from a Mrs. Myrtle Osborn in Houston, in which she claimed Billy had told her he thought his mother had been poisoned and expected the same would happen to him. But, if Billy had made such a statement he would probably have said the same thing to Isabelle Pope, and he did not. (See "Plot for Plot to be Fight in Shepherd Trial," *CDT*, 9 May 1925.)

CHAPTER 2: THE GRIFTERS

1. "Hang Shepherd, State Plea," *CDT*, 24 June 1925.
2. "Shepherd, Poor as Youth, Finds Friends Helpful," *CDT*, 14 March 1925.
3. "Hints 'Surprise' in Death Quiz on M'Clintock," *CDT*, 20 February 1925.
4. Federal census, 1880 and 1900; Indianapolis City Directory, 1890.
5. Unless otherwise indicated, details from William D. Shepherd's life come from his testimony at the trial. See "Shepherd's Life of Ease Pictured by State's Attorney," *CDT*, 24 June 1925 and "Shepherd a Witness, Denies Poisoning," *NYT*, 24 June 1925.
6. "Shepherd, Poor as Youth, Finds Friends Helpful," *CDT*, 14 March 1925; "Lack of Toil; Interest of Women Feature Story of Shepherd's Life," *CDT*, 18 March 1925.
7. "Seek Witnesses of Litigation over M'Clintock Wealth," *CDT*, 10 April 1925. The captain's quote is in "Shepherd, Poor as Youth, Finds Friends Helpful," *CDT*, 14 March 1925. This article says the captain's remark was made when he "testified in court," but doesn't specify what the cause of action was or how it concerned Shepherd.
8. Testimony of Isabelle Pope, in "M'Clintock-Pope Letters," 17 June 1925. Her statement never mentions Paul Dresser, but he is the author of the state song of Indiana.
9. "Seek Shepherd Clue in Fourth Death," *NYT*, 22 March 1925.
10. Ibid.
11. "Shepherd's Life of Ease Pictured by State's Attorney," *CDT*, 24 June 1925.
12. Ibid.
13. Information about Bethany College comes from its Web site at www.bethanylb.edu. Information about the Grafs and Emma Nelson comes from Sharon Bruce, Bethany College registrar.
14. Federal census for Saline County, Kansas, 1880. Peterson is listed as Robert Graf's nephew, but Graf was from Germany and Peterson's parents were born in Sweden. As Mrs. Graf and her parents were also born in Sweden, Peterson was most likely her nephew and not Mr. Graf's.

15. Federal census, 1870 and 1890; Doris Gregory, *History of Ouray: A Heritage of Mining and Everlasting Beauty*, vol. 1 (Ouray, CO: Cascade Publications, 1985). Nearly every mention of Carl Sigfrid in the newspapers during the Shepherd case indicates that he is Julie's brother or half-brother. On the stand, William Shepherd refers to him as his brother-in-law.

16. "Defense Gives Out Isabelle's Notes to Billy," *CDT*, 17 June 1925.

17. "Billy's Mother," *CDT*, 1 May 1925.

18. "Shepherd's Life of Ease Pictured by State's Attorney," *CDT*, 24 June 1925.

19. "Crowe Outlines State's Case," *CDT*, 12 June 1925.

20. Louis Kles: "Shepherd to Grand Jury Tomorrow," *CDT*, 15 March 1925; "Confesses to Typhoid Plot," *CDT*, 17 March 1925; Anna Anderson Beckford in James Doherty, "Tells New Tale of Shepherd's Microbe Quest," *CDT*, 14 June 1925.

21. James Doherty, "Tells New Tale of Shepherd's Microbe Quest," *CDT*, 14 June 1925.

22. "Bare Shepherd's Close Watch of Mrs. McClintock," *CDT*, 18 April 1925; "Billy's Mother," *CDT*, 1 May 1925.

23. "Bare Shepherd's," cited above.

24. "Delay Verdicts in McClintock Quiz until Today," *CDT*, 5 May 1925.

25. "Mrs. McClintock Servants Recite Gossip on Death," *CDT*, 17 April 1925 (Sigfrid); "Bare Shepherd's Close Watch of Mrs. McClintock," *CDT*, 18 April 1925 (adoption proposal).

26. "Crowe Outlines State's Case," *CDT*, 12 June 1925.

27. Probate file of the Estate of Emma McClintock; also "'Poison,' McClintock Report," *CDT*, 10 April 1925.

28. "Mrs. McClintock Servants Recite Gossip on Death," *CDT*, 17 April 1925.

29. "Witness Tells of M'Clintock Family Deaths," *CDT*, 27 February 1925; James Doherty, "Tells New Tale of Shepherd's Microbe Quest," *CDT*, 14 June 1925.

30. "Miss Pope Admits Deal for Fortune," *NYT*, 17 June 1925 (testimony of Leola Allard-Day).

31. "Quotes Queer Remark Made by Shepherd," *NYT*, 27 February 1925.

32. "Crowe Outlines State's Case," *CDT*, 12 June 1925.

33. "Witness Tells of M'Clintock Family Deaths," *CDT*, 27 February 1925 (Jerome Matillo); "Delay Verdicts in McClintock Quiz until Today," *CDT*, 5 May 1925 (Stella Costigan).

34. "Local Businessman Recalls Last Days of Famed Health Resort," *Lafayette-West Lafayette (IN) Journal & Courier*, 31 August 2003; see also the Warren County, Indiana, Community Network Web site at www. warrenco.net.

35. "'Killed for Greed'—Crowe," *CDT*, 12 June 1925.

36. Last will and testament of Emma Catherine McClintock.

37. "Delay Verdicts in McClintock Quiz until Today," *CDT*, 5 May 1925.

38. "Find Poison in Exhumed Bodies," *Decatur (IL) Daily Review*, 5 April 1925.

39. "Quotes Queer Remark Made by Shepherd," *NYT*, 27 February 1925.

40. "Hunt Germ Clews in Tombs," *CDT*, 27 March 1925.

41. "Mrs. McClintock Servants Recite Gossip on Death," *CDT*, 17 April 1925; "Describes Death of Mrs. M'Clintock," *NYT*, 5 May 1925; James Doherty, "Tells New Tale of Shepherd's Microbe Quest," *CDT*, 14 June 1925.

42. "Crowe Outlines State's Case," *CDT*, 12 June 1925.

43. Stella Costigan overheard Julie say this to Darl. In "Delay Verdicts in McClintock Quiz until Today," *CDT*, 5 May 1925.

44. Maureen McKernan, "Olson Stirs Inquest Anew," *CDT*, 7 January 1925.

45. These bills were submitted for payment by the estate of Emma McClintock and approved by the probate court. At the inquest, Alexander Reichmann testified that the estate was "substantially over a million dollars" when William McClintock Sr. died, but "substantially under a million dollars" when Emma died two years later. In "Rules on Shepherd Today," *CDT*, 24 March 1925.

46. "Delay Verdicts in McClintock Quiz until Today," *CDT*, 5 May 1925.

47. Estate of Emma C. McClintock.

48. "'Killed for Greed'—Crowe," *CDT*, 12 June 1925.

49. Ibid.

50. Ibid.

51. "Crowe Outlines State's Case," *CDT*, 12 June 1925; "Shepherd's Life of Ease Pictured by State's Attorney," *CDT*, 24 June 1925.

52. University of Michigan Law School records; Doris H. Gregory, *History of Ouray: A Heritage of Mining & Everlasting Beauty*, vol. 1 (Ouray, CO: Cascade Publications, 1985), 356–358.

53. Doris H. Gregory, 357; e-mail correspondence with Ouray County Historical Society; federal census for Ouray County, 1900 and 1910.

54. Doris H. Gregory, 357; e-mail correspondence with Ouray County Historical Society on Erin's last name; the 1920 and 1930 censuses list her as Sigfrid's wife, and her death certificate is in the name of Erin Sigfrid.

55. Correspondence with Ouray County Historical Society.

56. Gregory, 358.

57. Gregory, 358; e-mail correspondence with Ouray County Historical Society re: the claimed relationship.

58. Doris H. Gregory, *History of Ouray: Historical Homes, Buildings and People*, vol. 2 (Ouray, CO: Cascade Publications, 1985), 183.

59. "Millionaire Orphan Dead; About to Wed," *CDT*, 5 December 1924; "Hints 'Surprise' in Death Quiz on M'Clintock," *CDT*, 20 February 1925.

60. Dean Geroulis, "A Special Place for 2,500 People," *Chicago Tribune*, 4 April 2004.

61. Federal census for Cook County, 1910.

62. "Shepherd's Life of Ease Pictured by State's Attorney," *CDT*, 24 June 1925.

63. Ibid.

64. Doherty, "Tells New Tale of Shepherd's Microbe Quest," *CDT*, 14 June 1925.

65. "Shepherd Says Nurse Hounded Him for Money," *CDT*, 27 January 1925.

66. "McClintock Heir Returning," *CDT*, 26 December 1924.

67. Genevieve Forbes Herrick, "Isabelle Pope Tells Romance of McClintock," *CDT*, 24 December 1924.

68. "Hear Miss Pope's Own Story," *CDT*, 16 June 1925.

69. "Youth's View of Shepherds Told in Note," *CDT*, 17 June 1924: "Precious, I get out my little slip from Peacock's and look at it every now and then to be sure I still have it right with me. O, darling, what a glorious evening it will be when we put it on and wear it for the first time."

70. Ibid.

71. "M'Clintock-Pope Letters," *CDT*, 17 June 1925.

72. "Mrs. Shepherd Held to Jail," *CDT*, 6 May 1925 ("This marriage shall never take place"); "Hated Miss Pope Is Testimony," *Sheboygan (WI) Press*, 25 February 1925 ("Now we can keep her out"); "Says Shepherd Boasted about Future Riches," *CDT*, 26 February 1925.

73. "Says Shepherd Boasted about Future Riches," *CDT*, 26 February 1925.

74. "Billy's Mother," *CDT*, 1 May 1925. The judge said one woman was about forty and the other one about twenty-five, which closely coincides with the ages of Mrs. Davidson and her younger sister, Ruby Peel.

75. "Youth's View of Shepherds Told in Note," *CDT*, 17 June 1925.

76. Ibid.: "I have to have the Kenilworth house sold by next fall at the latest.... I can't see the $700 a month it costs to keep that darn place up.... [O]ne thing we must do is go over the entire house and pick out what we want. The rest to be stored or I'll give it to mother if she wants it."

77. "Get Shepherd Jury; Trial On," *CDT*, 11 June 1925.

78. "Wolff Delays Telling Tests on M'Clintock," *CDT*, 30 December 1924.

79. "Gorman Depicts Shepherd as Killer, Meriting Noose," *CDT*, 24 June 1925.

CHAPTER 3: THE AVENGING FURY AND
THE CONFIDENCE MAN

1. "Flaming Youth," in *The Jazz Age* (New York: Time-Life, Our American Century Series, 1998), 27–37.

2. "Suicide Ends Student's Ills," *CDT*, 13 April 1925; "Diary Reveals Plan of Youth to End His Life," *CDT*, 13 April 1925; Genevieve Forbes Herrick, "Student Death Held Warning for Parents," *CDT*, 14 April 1925; "Grave Is Setting for Last Act in Preston Tragedy," *CDT*, 15 April 1925; "Opinions Vary on Meaning of Preston Creed," *CDT*, 16 April 1925. Preston wrote this poem in December 1924:

> Wind tossed waves
> That seething, swirling,
> Foaming,
> Drive speedless onward,
> Breaking with thunderous roar;
> Hissing softly,
> As twinkling bubbles vanish
> Airily ...
> How soon thy force is spent
> And peacefully you lie
> Conquered by that
> Wave washed shore.
> O, moon swept beach,
> Would that I, too,
> Could let my troubles,
> Turbulent and unending,
> Sleep upon your silvery breast
> To be dispersed and lulled
> Into eternal rest.

3. Lois Gordon and Alan Gordon, *American Chronicle: Six Decades of American Life, 1920–1980* (New York: Atheneum, 1987), 43.

4. The best and most complete work on this case is Hal Higdon's *The Crime of the Century: The Leopold and Loeb Case* (New York: G. P. Putnam's Sons, 1975), reprinted in 1999 by University of Illinois Press and retitled *Leopold and Loeb: The Crime of the Century*. Maureen McKernan, a reporter for the *Chicago Herald & Examiner* and later the *Chicago Daily Tribune*, published *The Amazing Crime and Trial of Leopold and Loeb* in 1924 (Chicago: Plymouth Court Press), right after the case was completed. See Chapter 9, *infra*.

5. See Allan May, "Chicago's Unione Siciliana: 1920—A Decade of Slaughter (Part Four)," American Mafia Web site at www.americanmafia. com/Allan_May_10-15-00.html; and John W. Tuohy, "The Bloody Gennas," *Gambling Magazine Mob Stories* Web site at www.gamblingmagazine. com/articles/53/53-127.htm.

6. "St. Valentine's Day Massacre with Pictures—1929—Al Capone True Crime Story," at www.mysterynet.com/vdaymassacre.

7. Biographical information on Harry Olson comes from Northwestern University Archives (Harry Olson Papers); "Harry Olson Dies; Chicago Ex-Jurist," *NYT*, 2 August 1935; Scott Fornek, "Blind to a Nightmare," *Chicago Sun-Times*, 31 August 2003.

8. "Chicago Judge Beaten Up," *NYT*, 13 March 1920.

9. Russell Owen, "Undercurrents in the Shepherd Case," *NYT*, 21 June 1925.

10. "Open McClintock Death Quiz," *CDT*, 24 December 1924.

11. Maureen McKernan, "Olson Stirs Inquest Anew," *CDT*, 7 January 1925.

12. "Doctor Bares Shepherd's Poison Quest," *CDT*, 21 February 1925.

13. "'Killed for Greed'—Crowe," *CDT*, 12 June 1925.

14. "32 Dead in Christmas Fire," *CDT*, 25 December 1924; "School Ashes End Romance; Girl Is Dead, He's Dying," *CDT*, 26 December 1924.

15. Genevieve Forbes Herrick, "Isabelle Pope Tells Romance of McClintock," *CDT*, 24 December 1924.

16. "Shepherd Gives His M'Clintock Story to State," *CDT*, 28 December 1924.

17. Genevieve Forbes Herrick, "Chemist Testifies," *CDT*, 27 December 1924; "Germ Defense Coup Fails," *CDT*, 13 June 1925.

18. "'Indict Defamers'—Shepherd," *CDT*, 29 December 1924.

19. "Shepherd's Life of Ease Pictured by State's Attorney," *CDT*, 24 June 1925.

20. "Shepherd Tells of Care Given to McClintock," *CDT*, 25 December 1924. A reporter from the *Chicago Daily Tribune* went out to Albuquerque to interview Shepherd in the Davidson home: "Shepherd told of his leaving the practice of law for a short time in his early life in Kansas, when times were not prosperous. He studied pharmacy then, and became a licensed pharmacist, but worked at it only a few years."

21. "Shepherd Gives His M'Clintock Story to State," *CDT*, 28 December 1924.

22. "'Indict Defamers'—Shepherd," *CDT*, 29 December 1924.

23. "Typhoid Cases Total 99 since Late November," *CDT*, 1 January 1925.

24. Family of Isabelle Pope.

25. Maureen McKernan, "Olson Stirs Inquest Anew," *CDT*, 7 January 1925.

26. Ibid.

27. "Wm. A. [*sic*] Shepherd Made an Officer of His Church," *CDT*, 16 January 1925.

28. "Link Mrs. Shepherd with Two Murders," *NYT*, 6 May 1925.

29. "Open McClintock Death Quiz," *CDT*, 24 December 1924.

30. "Mrs. Shepherd Held to Jail," *CDT*, 6 May 1925.

31. Although this was alleged to have been in the letters by Miss Gehling, only four letters were introduced and only two of those released to the newspapers for printing. Neither of those two makes this statement. See "Hints 'Surprise' in Death Quiz on M'Clintock," *CDT*, 20 February 1925.

32. "Shepherd Says Nurse Hounded Him for Money," *CDT*, 27 January 1925.

33. Ibid.

34. "Denies Making Threats," *CDT*, 27 January 1925.

35. "Hints 'Surprise' in Death Quiz on M'Clintock," *CDT*, 20 February 1925.

36. Ibid.

37. "Shepherd's Life of Ease Pictured by State's Attorney," *CDT*, 24 June 1925.

38. "Witness Tells of M'Clintock Family Deaths," *CDT*, 27 February 1925. Shepherd's attorney objected to a question asked a witness by Judge Olson, and Olson caused some laughter in the courtroom when he said, "Objection overruled." The coroner who was presiding agreed with Olson's decision and Shepherd's attorney sarcastically commented, "I'll submit all my objections to him from now on."

39. "Rules on Shepherd Today," *CDT*, 24 March 1925.

40. "Doctor Bares Shepherd's Poison Quest," *CDT*, 21 February 1925.

41. "Shepherd Case Doctor Lands Sleuth in Jail," *CDT*, 22 February 1925.

42. "See Plot to Kidnap in M'Clintock Case," *NYT*, 23 February 1925.

43. "Guard McClintock Jury," *NYT*, 13 March 1925 (Clody); "Links Dr. Faiman to Death of Woman," *NYT*, 29 March 1925 (Olson).

44. "Witness Tells of M'Clintock Family Deaths," *CDT*, 27 February 1925.

45. "Seek Shepherd Name in Files of Germ School," *CDT*, 28 February 1925.

46. "Demands Faiman Be Court Witness," *CDT*, 18 June 1925.

47. Ibid.

48. "Seek Shepherd Name in Files of Germ School," *CDT*, 28 February 1925.

49. Ibid.

50. Karen Klinkenberg, University of Minnesota Archives.

51. Information from William Penn University Archives: *The History of Mahaska County, Iowa, 1984*, by the Keo-Mah Genealogical Society and Mahaska County Historical Society (Curtis Medi Corporation, 1985); Manoah Hedge, *Past and Present of Mahaska County* (Chicago: S. J. Clarke,

1906); Robert C. Scheetz, Drake University registrar, "Oskaloosa College, Oskaloosa, Iowa" (1981).

52. "Defense Rips into Faiman," *CDT*, 19 June 1925.

53. "Faiman a Puzzle to Police," *NYT*, 18 March 1925 ("acknowledged by men high in the medical profession to be one of the best bacteriologists in the country"); "Call Faiman's Science School a Quacks' Mill," *CDT*, 17 March 1925. ("Those who know Dr. Faiman best say that he is a good man and a scholar gone off on the wrong track. They say he is a genius when it comes to bacteriology—one of the best in the country—that he is qualified to teach it and has made some excellent bacteriologists of those who really wanted to learn.")

54. James Doherty, "Give Shepherd Drill before Taking Stand," *CDT*, 23 June 1925. Faiman listed himself as a physician in the 1920 and 1930 federal census, and this occupation is also on his death certificate.

55. Genevieve Forbes Herrick, "Faiman Called Opportunist by His Associates," *CDT*, 18 March 1925; "State's Germ Theory in Shepherd Case Assailed," *CDT*, 20 June 1925.

56. James Doherty, "Defense Rips into Faiman," *CDT*, 19 June 1925. On the stand, he told Crowe he was twenty-five, which was correct, but when he first spoke with the state's attorney and gave his confession, he said he was thirty ("Confession Made by Faiman," *NYT*, 18 March 1925). He also added five years when he reported his age to the census taker. Faiman was born in 1899.

57. "Call Faiman's Science School a Quacks' Mill," *CDT*, 17 March 1925.

58. Doherty, "Defense Rips into Faiman," *CDT*, 19 June 1925.

59. Herrick, "Faiman Called Opportunist by His Associates," *CDT*, 18 March 1925.

60. Ben Feller, Associated Press, "Investigation: 28 Top Federal Workers Have Bogus College Degrees," *Moscow (ID)—Pullman (WA) Daily News*, 11 May 2004. See also "Spokane a 'Hot Spot' for Dubious Degrees," *Moscow-Pullman Daily News*, 1 December 2003.

61. The four states are Oregon, North Dakota, New Jersey, and Illinois ("Spokane a 'Hot Spot' for Dubious Degrees," cited above).

62. "Schools Such as Faiman's Target of State Official," *CDT*, 24 March 1925.

63. Ibid.

64. James Doherty, "Rip Shepherd Defense with His Witnesses," *CDT*, 21 June 1925.

65. Ibid.; also Doherty, "Give Shepherd Drill before Taking Stand," *CDT*, 23 June 1925 and "Refuse Bail to Shepherd; in Cell No. 13," *CDT*, 19 March 1925.

66. Doherty, "State's Germ Theory in Shepherd Case Assailed," *CDT*, 20 June 1925.

67. "Links Dr. Faiman to Death of Woman," *NYT*, 29 March 1925.

68. History Link Database Output, http://www.historylink.org/_ output.cfm; see also Katha Pollitt's review of *When Abortion Was a Crime: Women, Medicine, and Law in the United States, 1867–1973* by Leslie J. Reagan (Berkeley: University of California Press, 1997) in *Atlantic Monthly*, May 1997, 111–115.

69. Unless otherwise stated, Faiman's encounters with Shepherd are taken from his testimony at the inquest ("Indict Shepherd and Faiman," *CDT*, 18 March 1925) and at the trial ("Defense Rips into Faiman," *CDT*, 19 June 1925).

70. "Waite Confesses to Two Murders," *NYT*, 29 March 1916; "Swope Poison Case Must Be Retried," *NYT*, 12 April 1911 (a good summary of the case).

71. The letter is published in *CDT*, 18 March 1925, under the heading "Letter Which Revealed Faiman's Hope for Wealth."

72. "Confession Made by Faiman," *NYT*, 18 March 1925.

73. "Germans Stolen, Shepherd Case Doctor Asserts," *CDT*, 1 March 1925.

74. "Dr. Faiman, on Grill, Admits Bacilli Taken," *CDT*, 13 March 1925; "Demands Faiman Be Court Witness," *CDT*, 18 June 1925.

75. "Dr. Faiman, on Grill, Admits Bacilli Taken," *CDT*, 13 March 1925.

76. James Doherty, "Tells New Tale of Shepherd's Microbe Quest," *CDT*, 14 June 1925.

77. "Defense Rips into Faiman," *CDT*, 19 June 1925.

78. "Confesses to Typhoid Plot," *CDT*, 17 March 1925.

79. "Indict Shepherd and Faiman," *CDT*, 18 March 1925.

80. "Seeks Writ for Faiman," *NYT*, 16 April 1925.

81. Doherty, "Defense Rips into Faiman," *CDT*, 19 June 1925.

82. "Rules on Shepherd Today," *CDT*, 24 March 1925.

83. "Draft Chicago Germ Ordinance as Result of Shepherd Case," *NYT*, 30 April 1925.

84. Doherty, "Defense Rips into Faiman," *CDT*, 19 June 1925.

CHAPTER 4: HIPPODROME

1. "Girl, 16, Kills Mother Because of Scolding," *NYT*, 16 January 1925; "Ellingson Girl Takes Conviction Calmly," *NYT*, 24 August 1925.

2. The best account of this case, including behind-the-scenes stories, is in Robert K. Murray and Roger W. Brucker, *Trapped! The Story of Floyd Collins* (University of Kentucky Press, 1982).

3. Tri-State Tornado Web page, www.crh.noaa.gov/pah/1925.

4. From *CDT* of 1 July 1925. In the 24 February 1925 edition, the fifty-fourth day of the year, the total was eighty-two for auto deaths, fifty-seven for guns, and thirty-five for moonshine. Not even a month

later, on 21 March, the count for auto deaths had gone up to 128, with guns at 86 and moonshine at 55. It was never stated how people died from "moonshine." They may have been drinking bad booze, or overindulging, or having auto accidents while escaping the law; or it may be that all alcohol-related deaths were being counted.

5. "Bar Raw Oyster Dishes in State after Jan. 15," *CDT*, 11 January 1925.

6. "Wife Stands by Shepherd; Says He Is Entirely Innocent," *CDT*, 18 March 1925; Genevieve Forbes Herrick, "Shepherd's Wife Charges Plot; Blames Gossip," *CDT*, 19 March 1925.

7. "Seize Shepherd and Wife," *CDT*, 14 March 1925.

8. Ibid.

9. "Shepherd Assigned to Murderers' Row," *NYT*, 20 March 1925.

10. Leo Koretz's colorful career is recounted in Dean Jobb, *Crime Wave: Con Men, Rogues, and Scoundrels from Nova Scotia's Past* (East Lawrencetown, NS: Pottersfield Press, 1995).

11. "Diary Reveals Plan of Youth to End His Life," *CDT*, 13 April 1925.

12. "Shepherd Back in Jail As Hearing Continues," *NYT*, 24 March 1925 (Julie's claim); "Links Dr. Faiman to Death of Woman," *NYT*, 29 March 1925 (Shepherd's claim).

13. John W. Tuohy, "The St. Paul Incident," on American Mafia Web site (www.americanmafia.com), August 2001.

14. "Noted Lawyer Shot in Chicago Gang War; 2 Killed, 3 Wounded," *NYT*, 12 October 1926.

15. Patricia Eliot Tobias, "The Old Razzle Dazzle," in *Written By* at www.wga.org/writtenby/0203/chicago.html (February 2003).

16. Genevieve Forbes Herrick, "Shepherds like Opposite Poles As Trial Opens," *CDT*, 19 May 1925.

17. "Next Step Is Fight over $1,000,000 Will," *CDT*, 27 June 1925.

18. Ibid.

19. "Toombs Lost Money Backing Shepherd in Murder Case," *Decatur (IL) Daily Review*, 27 September 1928; "Toombs Fund Helped Finance William Shepherd," *Decatur (IL) Herald*, 28 September 1928.

20. "Confesses to Typhoid Plot," *CDT*, 17 March 1925.

21. Nellie Bly was the pseudonym of Elizabeth Jane Cochrane (1864–1922), who, as a young journalist in the 1880s, went undercover inside Blackwell's Insane Asylum in New York City and exposed atrocities in her newspaper articles. See Brooke Kroeger, *Nellie Bly* (New York: Three Rivers Press, 1995).

22. *American Women: Women Reporters*, Library of Congress's American Memory Web site at http://memory.loc.gov/ammem/awhtml/awser2/women_reporters.html (12 November 2004).

23. Hal Higdon, *Leopold and Loeb: The Crime of the Century* (Urbana: University of Illinois Press, 1999), 263.

24. Genevieve Forbes Herrick, "'Darl' Is My Strength and Hope, Accused Wife of Shepherd Avows," *CDT*, 7 May 1925; "Mrs. Shepherd Freed on Bail; Sees Husband," *CDT*, 8 May 1925.

25. "False Report Made on Dr. Olson Death," *NYT*, 12 April 1925.

26. "Seek Shepherd Clue in Fourth Death," *NYT*, 22 March 1925.

27. "Mrs. Shepherd Held to Jail," *CDT*, 6 May 1925.

28. "Hiding over Night, McClintock's [*sic*] Wife Denounces Olson," *CDT*, 6 May 1925.

29. "Mrs. Shepherd Not to Surrender Now," *Sheboygan (WI) Press*, 6 May 1925.

30. "Bail for Shepherd Refused by Court," *NYT*, 26 March 1925.

31. Herrick, "Shepherds like Opposite Poles As Trial Opens," *CDT*, 19 May 1925.

32. "Germs Stolen, Shepherd Case Doctor Asserts," *CDT*, 1 March 1925.

33. "Shepherd Bail Plea Again in Court Today," *CDT*, 23 March 1925.

34. "Olson Rips into Shepherd," *CDT*, 4 March 1925.

35. "Both Sides Cry Germ Plot in Shepherd Case," *CDT*, 29 March 1925.

36. "Crowe Piles Up Evidence for Shepherd Trial," *CDT*, 2 May 1925; "Woman Witness Beaten," *CDT*, 8 May 1925.

37. "Crowe Piles Up Evidence," cited above.

38. "Try Again to Free Shepherd on Bail Today," *CDT*, 31 May 1925.

39. "Poison Adds New Shepherd Mystery," *CDT*, 6 April 1925; "Jury to Get Shepherd Case Today," *CDT*, 26 June 1925.

40. "Mercury Sure, Subtle Poison, Doctors Assert," *CDT*, 11 April 1925; Serita D. Stevens, *Deadly Doses: A Writer's Guide to Poisons* (Cincinnati: Writer's Digest Books, 1990), 216–218.

41. Edward Swallow, "Letter to the Editor," *NYT*, 26 June 1913.

42. "Crane Tech Boy Takes Own Life over Ill Health," *CDT*, 3 June 1925.

43. Swallow, "Letter"; William J. Robinson, MD, "Letter to the Editor," *NYT*, 16 June 1913.

44. "Say Step-Mother Sent Poison Candy to Child in Olean," *NYT*, 24 December 1924.

45. "Probe Shepherd Bribe Charge," *CDT*, 28 March 1925; "'Poison,' McClintock Report," *CDT*, 10 April 1925.

46. Ibid., and "Delay Verdicts in McClintock Quiz until Today," *CDT*, 5 May 1925.

47. "Billy's Mother," *CDT*, 1 May 1925.

48. "Link Mrs. Shepherd with Two Murders," *NYT*, 6 May 1925.

49. "No Poison Found in Olson's Body, Chemist Reports," *CDT*, 19 April 1925.

50. Edward C. Derr, United Press, Untitled Article, *Sheboygan (WI) Press*, 18 March 1925.

51. "Hiding over Night, McClintock's [*sic*] Wife Denounces Olson," *CDT*, 6 May 1925.

52. Herrick, "'Darl' Is My Strength and Hope, Accused Wife of Shepherd Avows," *CDT*, 7 May 1925; "Mrs. Shepherd Freed on Bail; Sees Husband," *CDT*, 8 May 1925.

53. Ibid.

54. "Let Mrs. Shepherd Go Home," *CDT*, 7 May 1925.

55. Herrick, "Mrs. Shepherd Freed on Bail; Sees Husband," *CDT*, 8 May 1925.

56. Ibid. See also federal census for Cook County, 1930, where Eva is listed as her daughter and is living in her household.

57. "Mrs. Shepherd Wins Freedom; Assails Olson," *CDT*, 14 May 1925.

CHAPTER 5: *THE STATE OF ILLINOIS V. WILLIAM DARLING SHEPHERD*

1. "State Stars in Shepherd Case Ready for Trial," *CDT*, 16 May 1925; Maureen McKernan, "Begin Shepherd Trial Today," *CDT*, 18 May 1925.

2. The ongoing saga of the missing witness, Robert White, can be found in *CDT* editions of 20, 21, 22, 25, 26, and 27 May 1925, and in *NYT*, 30 May 1925.

3. "'Killed for Greed'—Crowe," *CDT*, 12 June 1925.

4. The story of "Cal" Callan appears in *CDT* editions of 21–25 May 1925, and his quotes to Philip Barry appear in "Jury Fixing Talk in Shepherd Case," *Helena (MT) Independent*, 24 May 1925.

5. "Crowe Guards All Witnesses for Germ Trial," *CDT*, 25 May 1925.

6. Orville Dwyer, "Crowe Wars on Shepherd Defense Lawyers," *CDT*, 26 May 1925; "Murder Trial Witness Seized in 'Germ Case,'" *CDT*, 31 May 1925.

7. "Thus Are Juries Selected!" *NYT*, 30 May 1925. See also "An Abuse at Its Worst," editorial, *NYT*, 12 June 1925.

8. "Four Jurors Picked for Shepherd Trial," *NYT*, 19 May 1925.

9. "Scan 15 for Shepherd Jury," *CDT*, 19 May 1925.

10. "Shepherd Witness in Philadelphia," *NYT*, 26 May 1925.

11. Genevieve Forbes Herrick, "Swear in Four," *CDT*, 23 May 1925; "Accused Germ Case Fixer Held in $2,500 Bail," *CDT*, 24 May 1925.

12. "Assails Judge Olson at Shepherd Trial," *NYT*, 4 June 1925.

13. "Nurse Comes to Aid Shepherd Defense," *NYT*, 23 June 1925.

14. "Scan 15 for Shepherd Jury," *CDT*, 19 May 1925.

15. "Get Shepherd Jury; Trial On," *CDT*, 11 June 1925.

16. "Flyers Isolated in Arctic," *CDT*, 23 May 1925; "Amundsen Missing 112 Hours in Arctic," *NYT*, 26 May 1925.

17. Genevieve Forbes Herrick, "New Rich Rum Chief Slain by Gunmen in Car," *CDT*, 27 May 1925; "Chicago Ne'er Had Funeral Like Genna's," *CDT*, 30 May 1925.

18. John W. Tuohy, "The Bloody Gennas," in *Gambling Magazine Mob Stories* at http://www.gamblingmagazine.com/articles/53/53-127.htm.

19. "Richard Loeb, Franks Killer, Grows Violent," *CDT*, 6 June 1925; "Richard Loeb, Franks Killer, Called Insane," *CDT*, 7 June 1925.

20. "The Coal Glen Mining Disaster" at http://freepages.history.rootsweb.com/~pfwilson/coal_glen.html.

21. The "Monkey Trial" was held in June and July 1925; Bryan died in July while it was still going on. See "Dies During 'Monkey Trial,'" *CDT*, 28 July 1925.

22. "Suicide in Baby Carriage," *NYT*, 9 June 1925.

23. "Seeks to Bar Murderers from Victims' Estates," *CDT*, 10 May 1925; "Plan Bill in Illinois to Disinherit Slayers," *NYT*, 10 May 1925.

24. "Held for Slaying Sister," *NYT*, 8 October 1912.

25. "Legal Stage Set with Shepherd Trial Effects," *CDT*, 15 May 1925; "State Witness Is Missing," *Sheboygan (WI) Press*, 19 May 1925.

26. "Legal Stage Set," cited above.

27. "Judge Thomas Lynch of Illinois Court, 70," *NYT*, 11 July 1950.

28. "Summary of Indictment against Shepherd," *CDT*, 19 March 1925.

29. "Aconite," Alternative Medicine Web site at www.metromkt.net/riable/1aconite.shtml.

30. Stevens, *Deadly Doses*, 14–17.

31. Ibid., 14.

32. Ibid.

33. "Crowe Strikes New Trail of Jury Fixers," *CDT*, 29 May 1925.

34. Genevieve Forbes Herrick, "State's Charge of Panhandling Jars Shepherds," *CDT*, 12 June 1925.

35. Ibid. (Stewart: "They may have been none too energetic, even a bit lazy.")

36. "'Killed for Greed'—Crowe," *CDT*, 12 June 1925.

37. Ibid.

38. "Germ Defense Coup Fails," *CDT*, 13 June 1925.

39. "'Killed for Greed'—Crowe," *CDT*, 12 June 1925.

40. James Doherty, "Tells New Tale of Shepherd's Microbe Quest," *CDT*, 14 June 1925 (Sbarbaro); "Germ Defense Coup Fails," *CDT*, 13 June 1925 (bank cashier).

41. "Trace Typhoid Germ Sale for McClintock Quiz," 25 February 1925; "Germs Stolen, Shepherd Case Doctor Asserts," *CDT*, 1 March 1925.

42. "Real Estate Transfers," *Fayetteville (AR) Daily Democrat*, 3 March 1921.

43. "Germ Defense Coup Fails," *CDT*, 13 June 1925.

44. James Doherty, "Tells New Tale of Shepherd's Microbe Quest," *CDT*, 14 June 1925; Doherty, "Hear Miss Pope's Own Story," *CDT*, 16 June 1925.

45. Doherty, "Hear Miss Pope's," cited above; Doherty, "M'Clintock-Pope Letters," *CDT*, 17 June 1925.

46. Doherty, "Hear Miss Pope's," cited above.

47. Doherty, "M'Clintock-Pope Letters," *CDT*, 17 June 1925.

48. Family of Isabelle Pope.

49. James Doherty, "Hear Miss Pope's Own Story," *CDT*, 16 June 1925.

50. Indiana residents in the Spanish-American War, online database through Ancestry.com. William D. Shepherd is listed, but neither of his brothers are.

51. "Demands Faiman Be Court Witness," *CDT*, 18 June 1925.

52. Ibid.

53. "Defense Rips into Faiman," *CDT*, 19 June 1925.

54. "'Dr.' Faiman Recites Deal with Shepherd for Poison Germs," *NYT*, 19 June 1925.

55. Ibid.

CHAPTER 6: DEFENDING DARL SHEPHERD

1. "Two Trapped As They Try Perfect Crime," *CDT*, 28 June 1925; "Admit Fake Kidnapping," *NYT*, 30 August 1925; "Draw Light Terms," *Helena (MT) Independent*, 13 September 1925.

2. "'All a Plot'—Shepherd Plea," *CDT*, 25 June 1925; "Jury to Get Shepherd Case Today," 26 June 1925.

3. James Doherty, "State's Germ Theory in Shepherd Case Assailed," *CDT*, 20 June 1925.

4. James Doherty, "Rip Shepherd Defense with His Witnesses," *CDT*, 21 June 1925.

5. Ibid.

6. James Doherty, "Give Shepherd Drill before Taking Stand," *CDT*, 23 June 1925. Baron Munchausen was an eighteenth-century German soldier who concocted wild, improbable tales about his adventures. He is featured in a book by Rudolf Raspe (1785) and has become synonymous with stories too fantastic for belief. Munchausen's Syndrome and Munchausen's Syndrome by Proxy are recognized psychological disorders.

7. Ibid.

8. "Nurse Comes to Aid Shepherd Defense," *NYT*, 23 June 1925.

9. James Doherty, "Give Shepherd Drill before Taking Stand," *CDT*, 23 June 1925.

10. James Doherty, "State's Germ Theory in Shepherd Case Assailed," *CDT*, 20 June 1925.

11. "Hang Shepherd, State Plea," *CDT*, 24 June 1925.

12. "Shepherd's Life of Ease Pictured by State's Attorney," *CDT*, 24 June 1925.

13. "Gorman Depicts Shepherd as Killer, Meriting Noose," *CDT*, 24 June 1925.

14. Doherty, "'All a Plot'—Shepherd Plea," *CDT*, 25 June 1925.

15. "Shepherd Is Persecuted, Says Defense," *Waukesha (WI) Daily Freeman*, 24 June 1925.

16. "Crowe's Closing Argument for the State," *CDT*, 27 June 1925.

17. "Jury Divided As First Vote Is Discussed," *CDT*, 27 June 1925.

18. "Shepherd Acquitted in M'Clintock Case; Jury Out 5½ Hours," *NYT*, 27 June 1925. It's interesting to note that the *Chicago Daily Tribune*, while making a vague reference to "a demonstration as is seldom witnessed in any courtroom," gave no specific details, while out-of-town newspapers commented on the "bedlam" that ensued.

19. Ibid. Also "Shepherd Freed by His Peers," *Helena (MT) Independent*, 27 June 1925 ("Some had their dresses nearly ripped off").

20. Doherty, "Next Step Is Fight over $1,000,000 Will," *CDT*, 27 June 1925.

21. "Shepherd Cleared of All Charges," *NYT*, 28 June 1925; "Faiman Freed by Court after State's Motion," *CDT*, 30 June 1925.

22. "Unruly Crowds," editorial, *NYT*, 29 June 1925.

23. "Spirit Message Assures Mother of Wm. Shepherd," *Decatur (IL) Daily Review*, 27 June 1925.

24. "How Verdict Was Met by Chief Actors," *CDT*, 27 June 1925.

25. Ibid.

26. Ibid.

27. "Faiman Freed by Court after State's Motion," *CDT*, 30 June 1925.

28. Doherty, "Next Step Is Fight over $1,000,000 Will," *CDT*, 27 June 1925.

29. "Shepherd Case Dropped, but Faiman Is Held," *CDT*, 28 June 1925.

30. "Crowe Outlines State's Case," *CDT*, 12 June 1925. ("Faiman is counting his chickens before they are hatched. He gets in touch with architects to see what kind of a school he can put up for $100,000, and the architect will testify here on the stand.")

31. "Shepherd Case Dropped, but Faiman Is Held," *CDT*, 28 June 1925.

32. "Clew Fails As Woman Looks at W. D. Shepherd," *CDT*, 6 March 1925.

33. "Distrust of Faiman Held as Result of Verdict," *Waukesha (WI) Daily Freeman*, 27 June 1925; "No Evidence," *Decatur (IL) Daily Review*, 28 June 1925.

34. Hal Higdon, *Leopold and Loeb: The Crime of the Century* (Urbana: University of Illinois Press, 1999), 78.

35. Russell Owen, "Undercurrents in the Shepherd Case," *NYT*, 21 June 1925.

36. Editorial, *Waukesha (WI) Daily Freeman*, 27 June 1925.

37. "Shepherd Says He'll Sue Olson, Reichmann, Lee," *CDT*, 29 June 1925.

38. "Toombs Lost Money Backing Shepherd in Murder Case," *Decatur (IL) Daily Review*, 27 September 1928; "Toombs Fund Helped Finance William Shepherd," *Decatur (IL) Herald*, 28 September 1928.

CHAPTER 7: WAS IT OYSTERS OR MURDER?

1. Judith Miller, Stephen Engelberg, and William Broad, *Germs: Biological Weapons and America's Secret War* (New York: Simon & Schuster, 2001), 15–33.

2. Miller, Engelberg, and Broad, cited above, 35.

3. Manuel S. Peña, *Practical Criminal Investigation, Fifth Edition* (Incline Village, NV: Copperhouse Publishing Company, 2000), 129.

4. Sgt. Matthew K. McConnell, Wilmette (IL) Police Department.

5. Jacqueline Winspear, *Birds of a Feather* (New York: Soho Press, 2004), 107.

6. "Mrs. Shepherd Held to Jail," *CDT*, 6 May 1925.

7. Edward C. Derr, United Press, Untitled Article, *Sheboygan (WI) Press*, 18 March 1925.

8. "Says Shepherd Boasted about Future Riches," *CDT*, 26 February 1925.

9. "Interview Maid in Shepherd Case," *Havre (MT) Daily News Promoter*, 17 March 1925.

10. "Hated Miss Pope Is Testimony," *Sheboygan (WI) Press*, 25 February 1925.

11. "Shepherd Bail Plea Again in Court Today," *CDT*, 23 March 1925.

12. "Bare Shepherd's Close Watch of Mrs. McClintock," *CDT*, 18 April 1925.

13. Ibid.

14. "Describes Death of Mrs. M'Clintock," *NYT*, 5 May 1925.

15. "Mrs. McClintock Servants Recite Gossip on Death," *CDT*, 17 April 1925.

16. Family of Isabelle Pope.

17. Doherty, "M'Clintock-Pope Letters," *CDT*, 17 June 1925.

18. Ibid.

19. "State Stars in Shepherd Case Ready for Trial," *CDT*, 16 May 1925.

20. "Shepherd Pleads He Is Not Guilty," *NYT*, 17 April 1925. ("[Mrs. Beckford] described also the continuous influence of the Shepherds in every action of Mrs. McClintock, and declared Shepherd shaped Mrs. McClintock's every decision.")

21. *Macbeth*, act I, scene vii.

22. Correspondence with Ouray County Historical Society.

23. "Germs Stolen, Shepherd Case Doctor Asserts," *CDT*, 1 March 1925.

24. "Women, Stage, Gold Mine on Toombs' List," *Decatur (IL) Daily Review*, 16 October 1928.

25. "Shepherd's Life of Ease Pictured by State's Attorney's Questions," *CDT*, 24 June 1925.

26. *Queen v. Parker and Hulme* (New Zealand, 1954); Rupert Furneaux, *Famous Criminal Cases*, vol. 2 (London: Wingate, 1955), 32.

27. Idan Sharon, MD, et al., "Shared Psychotic Disorder," eMedicine Web site at www.emedicine.com/med/topic3352.htm (4 June 2004).

28. Hal Higdon, *Leopold and Loeb: The Crime of the Century* (Urbana: University of Illinois Press, 1999), 218.

29. Ibid., 225.

30. Idan Sharon, MD, cited above.

31. Ibid.

32. "Rules on Shepherd Today," *CDT*, 24 March 1925.

33. "Crowe Outlines State's Case," *CDT*, 12 June 1925.

34. "Tells How Shepherd Prevented Wedding," *NYT*, 16 June 1925.

35. "Confesses to Typhoid Plot," *CDT*, 17 March 1925.

CHAPTER 8: THE WILL CONTEST

1. "Million Dollar McClintock Will Fight on Today," *CDT*, 1 July 1925.

2. "'I Never Saw Typhoid Germ,'" *CDT*, 27 December 1924.

3. Estate of Emma C. McClintock.

4. Ibid.

5. Last will and testament of Emma McClintock (and holographic codicil).

6. In the 1900 census, Stella was twenty-three and living with her husband John and their infant daughter Maud. In the 1910 census, she and Maud were living in the Shepherd home and she indicated that she was a widow.

7. "Demands Faiman Be Court Witness," *CDT*, 18 June 1925.

8. "McClintock Heir Returning," *CDT*, 26 December 1924.

9. "Shepherd Gives His M'Clintock Story to State," *CDT*, 28 December 1924.

10. "Shepherd's Life of Ease Pictured by State's Attorney's Questions," *CDT*, 24 June 1925.

11. "Open McClintock Death Quiz," *CDT*, 24 December 1924.

12. "Interview Maid in Shepherd Case," *Elyria (OH) Chronicle Telegram*, 28 February 1925.

13. "Shepherd Is Assaulted in Court Corridor," *CDT*, 15 July 1925.

14. "Shepherd Faces Last Battle on the McClintock Will," *Sheboygan (WI) Press*, 15 July 1925.

15. "Says Shepherd Boasted about Future Riches," *CDT*, 26 February 1925.

16. "Refuses to Probate M'Clintock's Will," *NYT*, 18 July 1925; "Beat Shepherd in First Fight over $1,000,000," *CDT*, 18 July 1925.

17. "Reply on McClintock Will," *NYT*, 7 May 1927.

18. "Sues for 'Widow's Share,'" *NYT*, 9 September 1927.

19. "Shepherd Gets Half of M'Clintock Estate," *NYT*, 16 September 1929.

20. "Shepherd Gets Half of Estate of McClintock," *CDT*, 15 September 1929. Good summary of the will contest.

CHAPTER 9: EPILOGUE

1. Published by the Plymouth Court Press in Chicago, 1924. This book was reprinted in 1957 by New American Library.

2. Paul Sann, "Kill the Dutchman!" at www.killthedutchman.net/chapter_VIII.htm.

3. This book was reprinted in 2003 as a paperback by Kessinger Publishing.

4. See fiftieth-anniversary highlights at http://wgngold.com.

5. Paul Sann, "Public Enemy No. 1, 1929," in *The Lawless Decade* at www.paulsann.org/thelawlessdecade/new1929-1.html. (Capone to Herrick: "You know, lady, I'd rather the newspapers wouldn't print a line about me. That's the way I feel. No brass band for me.... All I ever did was supply a demand that was pretty popular.")

6. "Establishment of the WAAC," at http://army.mil/cmh-pg/books/wwii/Wac/ch02.htm.

7. American Women: Women Reporters, Library of Congress' American Memory Web site at http://memory.loc.gov/ammem/awhhtml/awser2/women_reporters.html.

8. Ibid.

9. Ibid.

10. "Judge Thomas Lynch of Illinois Court, 70," *NYT*, 11 July 1950.

11. "Scott's Life Saved by Insanity Verdict," *NYT*, 7 August 1925.

12. "Shepherd Case Lawyer Fights High Alimony," *CDT*, 5 September 1925. (O'Brien to court: "I haven't made a cent in the last six months. In fact, I've lost money. And before that, I never made over $8,000 a year.")

13. "Noted Lawyer Shot in Chicago Gang War; 2 Killed, 3 Wounded," *NYT*, 12 October 1926; "Chicago Police War upon Bandits," *NYT*, 14 October

1926. For the Roosevelt incident, see H. W. Brands, *T. R.: The Last Romantic* (New York: Basic Books, 1997), 720–721. Roosevelt was on his way to give a campaign speech and the bullet couldn't penetrate the manuscript in his pocket. Undaunted, but still in pain, he went on with the speech anyway, showing the crowd his bloodstained shirt and the bullet-riddled papers. Needless to say, this had a dramatic effect on his audience, but it wasn't enough to help him defeat Woodrow Wilson for the presidency.

14. "'Slander,' Says Gangster," *NYT*, 6 February 1927.

15. "Chicago Attorney Starts Third Party," *NYT*, 30 May 1932.

16. "Chase Sentenced to Life," *NYT*, 29 March 1935.

17. "Urges Illinois Court Punish 47 Lawyers," *NYT*, 9 July 1931.

18. John W. Tuohy, "The St. Paul Incident," American Mafia Web site at http://americanmafia.com (August 2001).

19. This entire article can be read online at http://antipolygraph. org/articles/article-034.shtml.

20. "Senate Subpoena Defied," *NYT*, 6 September 1950.

21. Hal Higdon, *Leopold and Loeb: The Crime of the Century* (Urbana: University of Illinois Press, 1999), 321–322.

22. *Harrison v. The Northern Trust* (1942) was for the recovery of alleged overpayment of estate taxes. The Supreme Court found for the taxpayer.

23. "Mrs. Lolita Armour Moves into New Home," *NYT*, 8 January 1931.

24. "Surgeon Sentenced to Die," *NYT*, 10 March 1928.

25. *People v. Rongetti* (1930) 331 Ill. 581, 163 N.E. 373; *People v. Rongetti* (1947) 395 Ill. 580.

26. Homicide in Chicago, 1870–1930, online at http://homicide. northwestern.edu.

27. Ancestry.com, Social Security Death Index, and federal census.

28. Stella Costigan had married Harry Carson at the time of the trial. Information also from federal census for 1930.

29. Anna Anderson had married Mr. Beckford at the time of the trial.

30. As a matter of fact, Kles has no paper trail *before* 1925, either, so it may be that Kles is a shortened version of his real name.

31. Scott Fornek, "Blind to a Nightmare," *Chicago Sun-Times*, 31 August 2003.

32. Illinois Death Index.

33. Federal census, Tarrant County, 1930. Faiman's son was born in Florida, so they obviously were there at some point, most likely right after leaving Chicago.

34. A young medical student at the University of Manitoba in the 1960s was doing research on abortion induction by drugs and chemicals from a historical perspective and found this reference in a book there. The reason it made an impression on him so that he was

able to remember it forty years later is that his own name is Charles Faiman! However, he is not related to the fake physician and didn't remember the title of the book where he found the reference.

35. Death certificate of Charles A. C. Faiman from Tarrant County Bureau of Vital Statistics.

36. Death certificate of Erin Sigfrid from Alameda County Bureau of Vital Statistics.

37. Doris Gregory, *History of Ouray: A Heritage of Mining and Everlasting Beauty*, vol. 1 (Ouray, CO: Cascade Publications, 1985), 356.

38. Doris Gregory, *History of Ouray: A Heritage of Mining and Everlasting Beauty*, vol. 2 (Ouray, CO: Cascade Publications, 1985), 181.

39. Family of Isabelle Pope.

40. "Isabelle Pope Married," *NYT*, 29 September 1929.

41. Family of Isabelle Pope.

42. Ibid.

43. Death certificate of Isabelle Harrington from California Bureau of Vital Statistics.

44. Federal census for Cook County, 1930.

45. Death certificate of William Darling Shepherd from Cook County Bureau of Vital Statistics.

46. Last will and testament of William Darling Shepherd.

47. Estate of William D. Shepherd.

48. Ridgewood Cemetery, Des Plaines, IL, records; death certificate for Julie Marie Gough; probate file of Julie Marie Gough.

Selected Bibliography

Bethany College (Lindsborg, Kansas) Archives.

California Death Index.

Cook County (IL) Circuit Court Clerk Archives.

Cook County (IL) Vital Statistics.

Dartmouth College Archives.

Federal census for Colorado, Illinois, Indiana, Kansas, New Mexico, Texas, Wisconsin.

Fornek, Scott. "Blind to a Nightmare." *Chicago Sun-Times*, 31 August 2003.

Furneaux, Rupert. *Famous Criminal Cases, Vol. 2*. London: Wingate, 1955.

Geroulis, Dean. "A Special Place for 2,500 People." *Chicago Tribune*, 4 April 2004.

Gordon, Lois, and Alan Gordon. *American Chronicle: Six Decades of American Life, 1920–1980*. New York: Atheneum, 1987.

Gregory, Doris H. *History of Ouray*, vols. 1 and 2. Ouray, CO: Cascade Publications, 1985.

Grossman, Kate N., and Rosalind Rossi. "At the Head of the Class." *Chicago Sun-Times*, 16 March 2003.

Higdon, Hal. *Leopold and Loeb: The Crime of the Century*. Urbana, IL: University of Illinois Press, 1999.

Homicide in Chicago, 1870–1930 (database). Online at http://homicide.northwestern.edu.

Hopkins (MN) High School Archives.

Illinois Death Index to 1950.

Illinois Regional Archives Depository.

Indiana Residents in the Spanish-American War. Online at Ancestry.com.

Jobb, Dean. *Crime Wave: Con Men, Rogues, and Scoundrels from Nova Scotia's Past*. East Lawrencetown, NS: Pottersfield Press, 1995.

Kroeger, Brooke. *Nellie Bly*. New York: Three Rivers Press, 1995.

McKernan, Maureen. *The Amazing Crime and Trial of Leopold and Loeb*. 1924. Reprint, New York: New American Library, 1957.

Miller, Judith, Stephen Engelberg, and William Broad. *Germs: Biological Weapons and America's Secret War*. New York: Simon & Schuster, 2001.

Murray, Robert K., and Roger W. Brucker. *Trapped! The Story of Floyd Collins*. Lexington, KY: The University Press of Kentucky, 1982.

New Trier Township (IL) High School Archives.

Northwestern University Archives.

Ouray County (CO) Historical Society Archives.

Peña, Manuel S. *Practical Criminal Investigation, Fifth Edition*. Incline Village, NV: Copperhouse Publishing Co., 2000.

Pollitt, Katha. Review of *"When Abortion Was a Crime: Women, Medicine, and Law in the United States, 1867–1973,"* by Leslie J. Reagan. *Atlantic Monthly*, May 1997, 111–115.

Sann, Paul. "Kill the Dutchman!" Online at http://www.killthedutchman.net/chapter_VIII.htm.

———. "Public Enemy No. 1, 1929." *The Lawless Decade*. Online at http://www.paulsann.org/thelawlessdecade/new1929-1.html.

Sharon, Idan, MD, et al. "Shared Psychotic Disorder." eMedicine Web site at http://www.emedicine.com/med/topic3352.htm (4 June 2004).

Stevens, Serita D., with Anne Klarner. *Deadly Doses: A Writer's Guide to Poisons*. Cincinnati: Writer's Digest Books, 1990.

Stewart, William Scott. "How to Beat the Lie Detector." Originally published in *Esquire Magazine*, 1941. Available online at http://antipolygraph.org/articles/article-034.shtml.

Tarrant County (TX) Vital Statistics.

Texas Death Index.

Time-Life Editors. *Our American Century: The Jazz Age*. New York: Time-Life, 1998.

Tobias, Patricia Eliot. "The Old Razzle Dazzle." *Written By*. Online at http://www.wga.org/writtenby/0203/chicago.html (February 2003).

Tuohy, John W. "The Bloody Gennas." *Gambling Magazine Mob Stories*. Online at http://www.gamblingmagazine.com/articles/53/53-127.htm.

———. "The St. Paul Incident." *America Mafia*. Online at http://www.americanmafia.com (August 2001).

University of Michigan Law School Archives.

University of Minnesota Archives.

Index

About the Author

VIRGINIA A. McCONNELL is a native of Syracuse, New York, and has degrees from The College of St. Rose, Purdue University, and Golden State University Law School. She currently teaches English, Literature, and Speech at Walla Walla Community College's Clarkston Center in Clarkston, Washington. Her other books include *Arsenic Under the Elms: Murder in Victorian New Haven* (Praeger, 1999) and *Sympathy for the Devil: The Emmanuel Baptist Murders of Old San Francisco* (Praeger, 2001).